Free Speech

Other Books in the Issues on Trial Series

Free Speech

Sylvia Engdahl, Book Editor

GREENHAVEN PRESS
A part of Gale, Cengage Learning

GALE
CENGAGE Learning™

Detroit • New York • San Francisco • New Haven, Conn • Waterville, Maine • London

GALE
CENGAGE Learning™

Christine Nasso, *Publisher*
Elizabeth Des Chenes, *Managing Editor*

For more information, contact:
Greenhaven Press
27500 Drake Rd.
Farmington Hills, MI 48331-3535
Or you can visit our Internet site at gale.cengage.com

LIBRARY OF CONGRESS CATALOGING-IN-PUBLICATION DATA

Free speech / Sylvia Engdahl, book editor.
  p. cm. -- (Issues on trial)
Includes bibliographical references and index.
ISBN-13: 978-0-7377-2791-3 (hardcover)
ISBN-10: 0-7377-2791-8 (hardcover)
1. Freedom of speech--United States. 2. Students--Civil rights--United States.
3. Internet--Censorship--United States. I. Engdahl, Sylvia.
KF4772.F737 2008
342.7308'53--dc22
                                                        2007035991

Printed in the United States of America
2 3 4 5 6 7 12 11 10 09 08

Contents

Chapter 1: Upholding Non-disruptive Free Speech in Schools

Chapter 2: Denying Free Speech in Official School Publications

Chapter 3: Affirming That Internet Pornography Cannot Be Banned Outright

Chapter 4: Schools May Suppress Student Speech That Advocates Use of Illegal Drugs

Foreword

The U.S. courts have long served as a battleground for the most highly charged and contentious issues of the time. Divisive matters are often brought into the legal system by activists who feel strongly for their cause and demand an official resolution. Indeed, subjects that give rise to intense emotions or involve closely held religious or moral beliefs lay at the heart of the most polemical court rulings in history. One such case was *Brown v. Board of Education* (1954), which ended racial segregation in schools. Prior to *Brown*, the courts had held that blacks could be forced to use separate facilities as long as these facilities were equal to that of whites.

For years many groups had opposed segregation based on religious, moral, and legal grounds. Educators produced heartfelt testimony that segregated schooling greatly disadvantaged black children. They noted that in comparison to whites, blacks received a substandard education in deplorable conditions. Religious leaders such as Martin Luther King Jr. preached that the harsh treatment of blacks was immoral and unjust. Many involved in civil rights law, such as Thurgood Marshall, called for equal protection of all people under the law, as their study of the Constitution had indicated that segregation was illegal and un-American. Whatever their motivation for ending the practice, and despite the threats they received from segregationists, these ardent activists remained unwavering in their cause.

Those fighting against the integration of schools were mainly white southerners who did not believe that whites and blacks should intermingle. Blacks were subordinate to whites, they maintained, and society had to resist any attempt to break down strict color lines. Some white southerners charged that segregated schooling was *not* hindering blacks' education. For example, Virginia attorney general J. Lindsay Almond asserted, "With the help and the sympathy and the love and respect of the white people of the South, the colored man has risen under that educational process to a place of eminence and respect throughout the nation. It has served him well." So when the Supreme Court ruled against the segregationists in *Brown*, the South responded with vociferous cries of protest. Even government leaders criticized the decision. The governor of Arkansas, Orval Faubus, stated that he would not "be a party to any attempt to force acceptance of change to which the people are so overwhelmingly opposed." Indeed, resistance to integration was so great that when black students arrived at the formerly all-white Central High School in Arkansas, federal troops had to be dispatched to quell a threatening mob of protesters.

Nevertheless, the *Brown* decision was enforced and the South integrated its schools. In this instance, the Court, while not settling the issue to everyone's satisfaction, functioned as an instrument of progress by forcing a major social change. Historian David Halberstam observes that the *Brown* ruling "deprived segregationist practices of their moral legitimacy. . . . It was therefore perhaps the single most important moment of the decade, the moment that separated the old order from the new and helped create the tumultuous era just arriving." Considered one of the most important victories for civil rights, *Brown* paved the way for challenges to racial segregation in many areas, including on public buses and in restaurants.

In examining *Brown*, it becomes apparent that the courts play an influential role—and face an arduous challenge—in shaping the debate over emotionally charged social issues. Judges must balance competing interests, keeping in mind the high stakes and intense emotions on both sides. As exemplified by *Brown*, judicial decisions often upset the status quo and initiate significant changes in society. Greenhaven Press's Issues on Trial series captures the controversy surrounding influential court rulings and explores the social ramifications of such decisions from varying perspectives. Each anthology highlights one social issue—such as the death penalty, students' rights, or wartime civil liberties. Each volume then focuses on key historical and contemporary court cases that helped mold the issue as we know it today. The books include a compendium of primary sources—court rulings, dissents, and immediate reactions to the rulings—as well as secondary sources from experts in the field, people involved in the cases, legal analysts, and other commentators opining on the implications and legacy of the chosen cases. An annotated table of contents, an in-depth introduction, and prefaces that overview each case all provide context as readers delve into the topic at hand. To help students fully probe the subject, each volume contains book and periodical bibliographies, a comprehensive index, and a list of organizations to contact. With these features, the Issues on Trial series offers a well-rounded perspective on the courts' role in framing society's thorniest, most impassioned debates.

Introduction

The freedom to express opinions without interference by the government is among the most fundamental rights of Americans. The First Amendment to the Constitution states that "Congress shall make no law . . . abridging the freedom of speech," and the Fourteenth Amendment extends this rule to state and local governments. Unlike the citizens of many other nations, people in the United States cannot be punished for saying what they think.

However, freedom of speech is not absolute; there are necessary exceptions to the rule. For example, no one has the right to endanger others by causing panic, such as by shouting "fire" in a crowded building when there is no fire—or by making joking remarks about bomb threats. Most of the exceptions are less obvious than this, and have been established by judicial action. This is not to say that Congress and local governments never pass laws restricting speech—or actions considered symbolic speech—for reasons considered important; on the contrary, they frequently do. The question is whether such laws are constitutional, and this is often decided only when they are challenged in court. Decisions concerning exceptions to the right to free speech are not simple, and the finest legal scholars in the nation often disagree about them. That is why cases that involve them usually end up in the Supreme Court.

The first free-speech case ever dealt with by the Supreme Court was *Schenck v. United States* in 1919, which upheld the conviction of Charles Schenck under the Espionage Act for publishing a leaflet opposing the World War I draft. The Court ruled that speech may be suppressed if it presents a "clear and present danger" of bringing about evils Congress has a right to prevent. Since then, there have been a number of landmark cases involving threats to national security, which the government does need to eliminate. However, for the past half-century the expression of mere opposition to the government has been protected speech; only speech that actually incites its forcible overthrow may be prohibited.

Although most Americans support the *principle* of free speech, they nevertheless tend to feel that words or actions offensive to them should be banned. For example, in 1989 the Supreme Court ruled that flag burning as a form of protest is protected by the Constitution, saying, "If there is a bedrock principle underlying the First Amendment, it is that government may not prohibit the expression of an idea simply because society finds the idea itself offensive or disagreeable." (This statement has since been quoted by the Court in other contexts, including the dissenting opinion in the 2007 case included in this book.) Many people are strongly opposed to flag burning and attempts have been made by Congress to amend the Constitution in order to ban it, though so far they have not succeeded.

Also offensive to many people are obscenity and pornography, which have traditionally been exceptions to freedom of speech. Until the mid-twentieth century it was taken for granted that these should not be tolerated. Obscenity is still outside the protection of the First Amendment except when viewed only in private homes, but the definition of what is obscene has changed; it now depends on local community standards and on whether the material in question lacks literary, artistic, political, or scientific value. Laws against child pornography, however, have been upheld by the Court on the grounds that it is of prime importance for the government to protect children.

One other class of speech that the Court has explicitly banned is defamatory speech—slander and libel. The conditions under which speech is considered to fall in these categories are complicated, but in general, people are not allowed to make false statements of fact about other individuals (although they can express personal opinions). Unlike most forms of speech, which the First Amendment protects only against government censorship, personal opinion and statement of fact are protected against lawsuits by private parties.

Still another legally established limitation of free speech concerns "fighting words": words that "by their very utterance inflict injury or tend to incite an immediate breach of the peace," as the Court defined them in the 1942 case *Chaplinsky v. New Hampshire*. Until comparatively recently, this was not a controversial issue. But during the past few decades there has been increasing concern over hate speech, derogatory speech directed against minorities, which many colleges and communities prohibit. Does hate speech fall under the "fighting words" limitation? Although many people maintain that it should, laws and campus codes against hate speech challenged in court have usually been struck down, for they have covered not only words that incite violence, but speech such as mere opinion that is protected under the First Amendment.

The Supreme Court has not made a specific general ruling on hate speech, but it has allowed examples of it that in most other countries would have been banned. In *Brandenburg v. Ohio* (1969) it ruled that the Ku Klux Klan had a right to call for the expulsion of African-Americans and Jews from the United States, even through the use of violence, as long as there was no intent to cause immediate violence or any likelihood of doing so. This precedent, known as the Brandenburg test, means that inflammatory speech and even advocacy of unlawful action cannot be punished unless such action is actually imminent.

In 1978 the predominantly Jewish community of Skokie, Illinois, enacted laws to prevent Nazi demonstrators from marching in the public square and distributing material that "promotes and incites hatred against persons by reasons of their race, national origin, or religion." In striking down these laws the Supreme Court stated, "It is better to allow those who preach racial hate to expend their venom in rhetoric rather than to be panicked into embarking on the dangerous course of permitting the government to decide what its citizens may say and hear." This embodies the basic principle underlying all decisions that rest on the First Amendment's guarantee of free speech. The framers of the Bill of Rights believed that it is wrong for the government to decide what citizens may say and hear, even when the majority of them agree that particular ideas are objectionable.

Nearly everybody agrees that hate speech is a bad thing. But most also feel that, troubling as it is to permit hate speech, government control of people's right to their own opinions would be even worse. So there are no easy answers, and like all exceptions to general rules, the setting of limits to speech must be judged case by case in the light of the specific situation each case involves. "It is an unfortunate fact of our constitutional system that the ideals of freedom and equality are often in conflict," wrote District Court Judge Avern Cohn in *Doe v. University of Michigan*, which struck down the university's speech code on grounds that it was too broad. "The difficult and sometimes painful task of our political and legal institutions is to mediate the appropriate balance between these two competing values."

Striking a balance between values that conflict is the basis of almost all cases that involve the First Amendment, including those described in this book—none of which were decided unanimously when the Supreme Court voted on them. The dissenting justices (judges) as well as the authors of the majority opinions made strong points. Not everyone was pleased by these cases' outcomes. But the precedents they set have had, or will have, significant impact on the legal status of the free speech issues they raised.

CHAPTER 1

Upholding Non-disruptive Free Speech in Schools

Case Overview

Tinker v. Des Moines Independent Community School District (1969)

In 1965 opposition to the war in Vietnam was beginning to grow, and students on college campuses were demonstrating against it. Shortly before Christmas, on returning from an antiwar march in Washington, a small group of people met in Des Moines, Iowa, and agreed that they wanted to publicly express their conscientious objection to the war in a symbolic, nonviolent way. The group included high school students Christopher Eckhardt and John Tinker and their families. These students, along with John's sister Mary Beth and a few others, agreed to wear black armbands to school.

Another student decided to write an article for the school newspaper about the plan. This alerted school officials, and although the article was not published, the school board decided to ban the armbands because of the possibility of disturbance. It was announced that students who wore them would be suspended until they took them off. Christopher Eckhardt and John Tinker, who attended different high schools, and Mary Beth Tinker, who was in the eighth grade, all defied the ban and were sent home. They did not remove their armbands and return to school until after winter vacation. Meanwhile, there had been heated school board meetings attended not only by the students and their parents but by the media and a representative of the Iowa Civil Liberties Union. When it became clear that the board would not lift the ban, the Tinkers and Eckhardt, through their fathers, filed a suit in federal court on grounds that their constitutional right to free speech had been violated.

At the trial the attorneys for the school contended that the students were mere pawns of adults involved in the antiwar movement—that they had been put up to their protest either by the SDS (Students for a Democratic Society, a group of college-age radicals) or by their parents, who were known to be political activists. The students maintained that their parents had not tried to convince them to wear the armbands, although they had been supportive; they were expressing their own convictions. However, the district court held that the school's rule was reasonable, and on appeal the circuit court was evenly split, allowing the district court's decision to stand and increasing the chances that the Supreme Court would agree to review the case.

The resulting 1969 Supreme Court decision is a landmark in American law. It is the standard by which all subsequent student free speech cases have been judged; the "Tinker Test" has been applied many times and is still the overriding precedent today. The principle established by it—that students do not "shed their constitutional rights to freedom of speech or expression at the schoolhouse gate," as Justice Abe Fortas famously stated—has been modified by the decisions in several later cases, but departures from it are still considered exceptions.

The essence of the *Tinker* standard is that schools cannot suppress student speech, or symbolic expression equivalent to speech, unless not to do so would result in disruption of the work of the school or the rights of other students. The Court determined that the wearing of black armbands had not caused any such disruption. The school officials' mere fear that it would was not sufficient cause for imposing a ban. "Any word spoken, in class, in the lunchroom, or on the campus, that deviates from the views of another person may start an argument or cause a disturbance," Justice Fortas wrote. "But our Constitution says we must take this risk."

> "It can hardly be argued that either students or teachers shed their constitutional rights to freedom of speech or expression at the schoolhouse gate."

The Court's Decision: Students Have Fundamental Rights That Cannot Be Denied Under the Constitution

Abe Fortas

Abe Fortas was a justice of the Supreme Court from 1965 until 1969. Previously, as an attorney, he won the Supreme Court case that guarantees the right of criminal defendants to receive legal counsel even if they cannot afford to pay a lawyer. On the Supreme Court, Justice Fortas was known for his defense of children's rights. The following selection is the opinion he delivered in the case of Tinker v. Des Moines School District. *In it he explains why the Court ruled that students could not be punished for wearing black armbands at school to protest against the war in Vietnam. Armbands are a symbolic form of speech, he says, and the right to free speech cannot be denied merely because school officials fear disturbance, as long as no disorder or disruption of school activities actually occurs. Moreover, the school did not prohibit the wearing of other political or controversial symbols, and it clearly had no right to suppress one particular viewpoint.*

Abe Fortas, majority opinion, *Tinker et al. v. Des Moines Independent Community School District et al.*, U.S. Supreme Court, February 24, 1969.

Petitioner John F. Tinker, 15 years old, and petitioner Christopher Eckhardt, 16 years old, attended high schools in Des Moines, Iowa. Petitioner Mary Beth Tinker, John's sister, was a 13-year-old student in junior high school.

In December 1965, a group of adults and students in Des Moines held a meeting at the Eckhardt home. The group determined to publicize their objections to the hostilities in Vietnam and their support for a truce by wearing black armbands during the holiday season and by fasting on December 16 and New Year's Eve. Petitioners and their parents had previously engaged in similar activities, and they decided to participate in the program.

The principals of the Des Moines schools became aware of the plan to wear armbands. On December 14, 1965, they met and adopted a policy that any student wearing an armband to school would be asked to remove it, and if he refused he would be suspended until he returned without the armband. Petitioners were aware of the regulation that the school authorities adopted.

On December 16, Mary Beth and Christopher wore black armbands to their schools. John Tinker wore his armband the next day. They were all sent home and suspended from school until they would come back without their armbands. They did not return to school until after the planned period for wearing armbands had expired—that is, until after New Year's Day.

This complaint was filed in the United States District Court by petitioners, through their fathers. . . . After an evidentiary hearing the District Court dismissed the complaint. It upheld the constitutionality of the school authorities' action on the ground that it was reasonable in order to prevent disturbance of school discipline. The court referred to but expressly declined to follow the Fifth Circuit's holding in a similar case that the wearing of symbols like the armbands cannot be prohibited unless it "materially and substantially interfere[s] with the requirements of appropriate discipline in the operation of the school." *Burnside v. Byars.*

On appeal, the Court of Appeals for the Eighth Circuit considered the case en banc. The court was equally divided, and the District Court's decision was accordingly affirmed, without opinion.

Wearing Armbands Is Symbolic Speech

The District Court recognized that the wearing of an armband for the purpose of expressing certain views is the type of symbolic act that is within the Free Speech Clause of the First Amendment. As we shall discuss, the wearing of armbands in the circumstances of this case was entirely divorced from actually or potentially disruptive conduct by those participating in it. It was closely akin to "pure speech" which, we have repeatedly held, is entitled to comprehensive protection under the First Amendment.

First Amendment rights, applied in light of the special characteristics of the school environment, are available to teachers and students. It can hardly be argued that either students or teachers shed their constitutional rights to freedom of speech or expression at the schoolhouse gate. This has been the unmistakable holding of this Court for almost 50 years. In *Meyer v. Nebraska*, and *Bartels v. Iowa*, this Court, in opinions by Mr. Justice McReynolds, held that the Due Process Clause of the Fourteenth Amendment prevents States from forbidding the teaching of a foreign language to young students. Statutes to this effect, the Court held, unconstitutionally interfere with the liberty of teacher, student, and parent.

In *West Virginia v. Barnette*, this Court held that under the First Amendment, the student in public school may not be compelled to salute the flag. Speaking through Mr. Justice Jackson, the Court said:

> The Fourteenth Amendment, as now applied to the States, protects the citizen against the State itself and all of its crea-

tures—Boards of Education not excepted. These have, of course, important, delicate, and highly discretionary functions, but none that they may not perform within the limits of the Bill of Rights. That they are educating the young for citizenship is reason for scrupulous protection of Constitutional freedoms of the individual, if we are not to strangle the free mind at its source and teach youth to discount important principles of our government as mere platitudes.

On the other hand, the Court has repeatedly emphasized the need for affirming the comprehensive authority of the States and of school officials, consistent with fundamental constitutional safeguards, to prescribe and control conduct in the schools. Our problem lies in the area where students in the exercise of First Amendment rights collide with the rules of the school authorities.

Fear of Disturbance Is Not Enough to Overcome Rights

The problem posed by the present case does not relate to regulation of the length of skirts or the type of clothing, to hair style, or deportment. It does not concern aggressive, disruptive action or even group demonstrations. Our problem involves direct, primary First Amendment rights akin to "pure speech."

The school officials banned and sought to punish petitioners for a silent, passive expression of opinion, unaccompanied by any disorder or disturbance on the part of petitioners. There is here no evidence whatever of petitioners' interference, actual or nascent, with the schools' work or of collision with the rights of other students to be secure and to be let alone. Accordingly, this case does not concern speech or action that intrudes upon the work of the schools or the rights of other students.

Only a few of the 18,000 students in the school system wore the black armbands. Only five students were suspended for wearing them. There is no indication that the work of the schools or any class was disrupted. Outside the classrooms, a few students made hostile remarks to the children wearing armbands, but there were no threats or acts of violence on school premises.

The District Court concluded that the action of the school authorities was reasonable because it was based upon their fear of a disturbance from the wearing of the armbands. But, in our system, undifferentiated fear or apprehension of disturbance is not enough to overcome the right to freedom of expression. Any departure from absolute regimentation may cause trouble. Any variation from the majority's opinion may inspire fear. Any word spoken, in class, in the lunchroom, or on the campus, that deviates from the views of another person may start an argument or cause a disturbance. But our Constitution says we must take this risk, and our history says that it is this sort of hazardous freedom—this kind of openness—that is the basis of our national strength and of the independence and vigor of Americans who grow up and live in this relatively permissive, often disputatious, society.

In order for the State in the person of school officials to justify prohibition of a particular expression of opinion, it must be able to show that its action was caused by something more than a mere desire to avoid the discomfort and unpleasantness that always accompany an unpopular viewpoint. Certainly where there is no finding and no showing that engaging in the forbidden conduct would "materially and substantially interfere with the requirements of appropriate discipline in the operation of the school," the prohibition cannot be sustained. *Burnside v. Byars.*

In the present case, the District Court made no such finding, and our independent examination of the record fails to yield evidence that the school authorities had reason to anticipate that the wearing of the armbands would substantially interfere with the work of the school or impinge upon the rights of other students. Even an official memorandum prepared after the suspension that listed the reasons for the ban on wearing the armbands made no reference to the anticipation of such disruption.

On the contrary, the action of the school authorities appears to have been based upon an urgent wish to avoid the controversy which might result from the expression, even by the silent symbol of armbands, of opposition to this Nation's part in the conflagration in Vietnam. It is revealing, in this respect, that the meeting at which the school principals decided to issue the contested regulation was called in response to a student's statement to the journalism teacher in one of the schools that he wanted to write an article on Vietnam and have it published in the school paper. (The student was dissuaded.)

The School Did Not Prohibit Other Controversial Symbols

It is also relevant that the school authorities did not purport to prohibit the wearing of all symbols of political or controversial significance. The record shows that students in some of the schools wore buttons relating to national political campaigns, and some even wore the Iron Cross, traditionally a symbol of Nazism. The order prohibiting the wearing of armbands did not extend to these. Instead, a particular symbol— black armbands worn to exhibit opposition to this Nation's involvement in Vietnam—was singled out for prohibition. Clearly, the prohibition of expression of one particular opinion, at least without evidence that it is necessary to avoid material and substantial interference with schoolwork or discipline, is not constitutionally permissible.

In our system, state-operated schools may not be enclaves of totalitarianism. School officials do not possess absolute authority over their students. Students in school as well as out of school are "persons" under our Constitution. They are possessed of fundamental rights which the State must respect, just as they themselves must respect their obligations to the State. In our system, students may not be regarded as closed-circuit recipients of only that which the State chooses to communicate. They may not be confined to the expression of those sentiments that are officially approved. In the absence of a specific showing of constitutionally valid reasons to regulate their speech, students are entitled to freedom of expression of their views. As Judge Gewin, speaking for the Fifth Circuit, said, school officials cannot suppress "expressions of feelings with which they do not wish to contend." *Burnside v. Byars.*

In *Meyer v. Nebraska*, Mr. Justice McReynolds expressed this Nation's repudiation of the principle that a State might so conduct its schools as to "foster a homogeneous people." He said:

> In order to submerge the individual and develop ideal citizens, Sparta assembled the males at seven into barracks and intrusted their subsequent education and training to official guardians. Although such measures have been deliberately approved by men of great genius, their ideas touching the relation between individual and State were wholly different from those upon which our institutions rest; and it hardly will be affirmed that any legislature could impose such restrictions upon the people of a State without doing violence to both letter and spirit of the Constitution.

This principle has been repeated by this Court on numerous occasions during the intervening years. In *Keyishian v. Board of Regents*, Mr. Justice Brennan, speaking for the Court, said:

> 'The vigilant protection of constitutional freedoms is nowhere more vital than in the community of American schools.' *Shelton v. Tucker.* The classroom is peculiarly the 'marketplace of ideas.' The Nation's future depends upon leaders trained through wide exposure to that robust ex-

change of ideas which discovers truth 'out of a multitude of tongues, [rather] than through any kind of authoritative selection.'

The Students Did Not Cause Disruption of School Activities

The principle of these cases is not confined to the supervised and ordained discussion which takes place in the classroom. The principal use to which the schools are dedicated is to accommodate students during prescribed hours for the purpose of certain types of activities. Among those activities is personal intercommunication among the students. This is not only an inevitable part of the process of attending school; it is also an important part of the educational process. A student's rights, therefore, do not embrace merely the classroom hours. When he is in the cafeteria, or on the playing field, or on the campus during the authorized hours, he may express his opinions, even on controversial subjects like the conflict in Vietnam, if he does so without "materially and substantially interfer[ing] with the requirements of appropriate discipline in the operation of the school" and without colliding with the rights of others. *Burnside v. Byars.* But conduct by the student, in class or out of it, which for any reason—whether it stems from time, place, or type of behavior—materially disrupts classwork or involves substantial disorder or invasion of the rights of others is, of course, not immunized by the constitutional guarantee of freedom of speech.

Under our Constitution, free speech is not a right that is given only to be so circumscribed that it exists in principle but not in fact. Freedom of expression would not truly exist if the right could be exercised only in an area that a benevolent government has provided as a safe haven for crackpots. The Constitution says that Congress (and the States) may not abridge the right to free speech. This provision means what it says. We properly read it to permit reasonable regulation of speech-connected activities in carefully restricted circumstances. But we do not confine the permissible exercise of First Amendment rights to a telephone booth or the four corners of a pamphlet, or to supervised and ordained discussion in a school classroom.

If a regulation were adopted by school officials forbidding discussion of the Vietnam conflict, or the expression by any student of opposition to it anywhere on school property except as part of a prescribed classroom exercise, it would be obvious that the regulation would violate the constitutional rights of students, at least if it could not be justified by a showing that the students' activities would materially and substantially disrupt the work and discipline of the school. In the circumstances of the present case, the prohibition of the silent, passive "witness of the armbands," as one of the children called it, is no less offensive to the Constitution's guarantees.

As we have discussed, the record does not demonstrate any facts which might reasonably have led school authorities to forecast substantial disruption of or material interference with school activities, and no disturbances or disorders on the school premises in fact occurred. These petitioners merely went about their ordained rounds in school. Their deviation consisted only in wearing on their sleeve a band of black cloth, not more than two inches wide. They wore it to exhibit their disapproval of the Vietnam hostilities and their advocacy of a truce, to make their views known, and, by their example, to influence others to adopt them. They neither interrupted school activities nor sought to intrude in the school affairs or the lives of others. They caused discussion outside of the classrooms, but no interference with work and no disorder. In the circumstances, our Constitution does not permit officials of the State to deny their form of expression.

We express no opinion as to the form of relief which should be granted, this being a matter for the lower courts to determine. We reverse and remand for further proceedings consistent with this opinion.

> *"One does not need to be a prophet . . . to know that after the Court's holding today some students in Iowa schools and indeed in all schools will be ready, able, and willing to defy their teachers on practically all orders."*

Dissenting Opinion: Students Are Sent to School to Learn, Not to Broadcast Their Views to Others

Hugo Black

Hugo Black, previously a U.S. senator from Alabama, was a justice of the Supreme Court from 1937 to 1971. He is considered one of the most influential members of the Court in the twentieth century, and was noted for his strict, literal interpretation of the Constiution. The following viewpoint is his dissenting opinion in the case of Tinker v. Des Moines School District. *He argues that when students wore black armbands to school in protest against the war in Vietnam, it distracted others from their work, even though the majority of the Court felt that it caused no disruption of the school. Furthermore, he says, it is not true that any person has a constitutional right to go anywhere and express whatever ideas that person chooses, contrary to the rules of the place—for example, there is no such right in a church or a courtroom. In his opinion, the purpose of schools is for teachers to teach and students to learn, and therefore rules are necessary. In the opinion of Justice Black, the decision of the Court "sub-*

Hugo Black, dissenting opinion, *Tinker et al. v. Des Moines Independent Community School District et al.*, U.S. Supreme Court, February 24, 1969.

jects all the public schools in the country to the whims and ca-prices of their loudest-mouthed, but maybe not their brightest, students."

The Court's holding in this case ushers in what I deem to be an entirely new era in which the power to control pu-pils by the elected "officials of state supported public schools . . ." in the United States is in ultimate effect transferred to the Supreme Court. . . .

As I read the Court's opinion it relies upon the following grounds for holding unconstitutional the judgment of the Des Moines school officials and the two courts below. First, the Court concludes that the wearing of armbands is "symbolic speech" which is "akin to 'pure speech'" and therefore pro-tected by the First and Fourteenth Amendments. Secondly, the Court decides that the public schools are an appropriate place to exercise "symbolic speech" as long as normal school func-tions are not "unreasonably" disrupted. Finally, the Court ar-rogates to itself, rather than to the State's elected officials charged with running the schools, the decision as to which school disciplinary regulations are "reasonable."

Assuming that the Court is correct in holding that the conduct of wearing armbands for the purpose of conveying political ideas is protected by the First Amendment, cf., the crucial remaining questions are whether students and teachers may use the schools at their whim as a platform for the exer-cise of free speech—"symbolic" or "pure"—and whether the courts will allocate to themselves the function of deciding how the pupils' school day will be spent. While I have always believed that under the First and Fourteenth Amendments neither the State nor the Federal Government has any author-ity to regulate or censor the content of speech, I have never believed that any person has a right to give speeches or engage in demonstrations where he pleases and when he pleases. This Court has already rejected such a notion. In *Cox v. Louisiana*, for example, the Court clearly stated that the rights of free speech and assembly "do not mean that everyone with opinions or beliefs to express may address a group at any public place and at any time."

The Armbands Distracted Students from Schoolwork

While the record does not show that any of these armband students shouted, used profane language, or were violent in any manner, detailed testimony by some of them shows their armbands caused comments, warnings by other students, the poking of fun at them, and a warning by an older football player that other, nonprotesting students had better let them alone. There is also evidence that a teacher of mathematics had his lesson period practically "wrecked" chiefly by disputes with Mary Beth Tinker, who wore her armband for her "demonstration." Even a casual reading of the record shows that this armband did divert students' minds from their regular lessons, and that talk, comments, etc., made John Tinker "self-conscious" in attending school with his armband. While the absence of obscene remarks or boisterous and loud disorder perhaps justifies the Court's statement that the few armband students did not actually "disrupt" the classwork, I think the record overwhelmingly shows that the armbands did exactly what the elected school officials and principals foresaw they would, that is, took the students' minds off their classwork and diverted them to thoughts about the highly emotional subject of the Vietnam war. And I repeat that if the time has come when pupils of state-supported schools, kindergartens, grammar schools, or high schools, can defy and flout orders of school officials to keep their minds on their own schoolwork, it is the beginning of a new revolutionary era of permissiveness in this country fostered by the judiciary. The next logical step, it appears to me, would be to hold unconstitutional laws that bar pupils under 21 or 18 from voting, or from being elected members of the boards of education. . . .

I deny..., that it has been the "unmistakable holding of this Court for almost 50 years" that "students" and "teachers" take with them into the "schoolhouse gate" constitutional rights to "freedom of speech or expression." Even Meyer [*Meyer v. Nebraska*] did not hold that. It makes no reference to "symbolic speech" at all; what it did was to strike down as "unreasonable" and therefore unconstitutional a Nebraska law barring the teaching of the German language before the children reached the eighth grade. One can well agree with Mr. Justice Holmes and Mr. Justice Sutherland, as I do, that such a law was no more unreasonable than it would be to bar the teaching of Latin and Greek to pupils who have not reached the eighth grade. In fact, I think the majority's reason for invalidating the Nebraska law was that it did not like it or in legal jargon that it "shocked the Court's conscience," "offended its sense of justice," or was "contrary to fundamental concepts of the English-speaking world," as the Court has sometimes said. The truth is that a teacher of kindergarten, grammar school, or high school pupils no more carries into a school with him a complete right to freedom of speech and expression than an anti-Catholic or anti-Semite carries with him a complete freedom of speech and religion into a Catholic church or Jewish synagogue. Nor does a person carry with him into the United States Senate or House, or into the Supreme Court, or any other court, a complete constitutional right to go into those places contrary to their rules and speak his mind on any subject he pleases. It is a myth to say that any person has a constitutional right to say what he pleases, where he pleases, and when he pleases. Our Court has decided precisely the opposite.

Students Are Sent to School to Learn

In my view, teachers in state-controlled public schools are hired to teach there. Although Mr. Justice McReynolds may have intimated to the contrary in *Meyer v. Nebraska*, certainly a teacher is not paid to go into school and teach subjects the State does not hire him to teach as a part of its selected curriculum. Nor are public school students sent to the schools at public expense to broadcast political or any other views to educate and inform the public. The original idea of schools, which I do not believe is yet abandoned as worthless or out of date, was that children had not yet reached the point of experience and wisdom which enabled them to teach all of their elders. It may be that the Nation has outworn the old-fashioned slogan that "children are to be seen not heard," but one may, I hope, be permitted to harbor the thought that taxpayers send children to school on the premise that at their age they need to learn, not teach.

The true principles on this whole subject were in my judgment spoken by Mr. Justice McKenna for the Court in *Waugh v. Mississippi University.* . . . The State had there passed a law barring students from peaceably assembling in Greek letter fraternities and providing that students who joined them could be expelled from school. This law would appear on the surface to run afoul of the First Amendment's freedom of assembly clause. The law was attacked as violative of due process and of the privileges and immunities clause and as a deprivation of property and of liberty, under the Fourteenth Amendment. It was argued that the fraternity made its members more moral, taught discipline, and inspired its members to study harder and to obey better the rules of discipline and order. This Court rejected all the "fervid" pleas of the fraternities' advocates and decided unanimously against these Fourteenth Amendment arguments. The Court in its next to the last paragraph made this statement which has complete relevance for us today:

> It is said that the fraternity to which complainant belongs is a moral and of itself a disciplinary force. This need not be denied. But whether such membership makes against discipline was for the State of Mississippi to determine. It is to

be remembered that the University was established by the State and is under the control of the State, and the enactment of the statute may have been induced by the opinion that membership in the prohibited societies divided the attention of the students and distracted from that singleness of purpose which the State desired to exist in its public educational institutions. It is not for us to entertain conjectures in opposition to the views of the State and annul its regulations upon disputable considerations of their wisdom or necessity.

It was on the foregoing argument that this Court sustained the power of Mississippi to curtail the First Amendment's right of peaceable assembly. And the same reasons are equally applicable to curtailing in the States' public schools the right to complete freedom of expression. Iowa's public schools, like Mississippi's university, are operated to give students an opportunity to learn, not to talk politics by actual speech, or by "symbolic" speech. And, as I have pointed out before, the record amply shows that public protest in the school classes against the Vietnam war "distracted from that singleness of purpose which the State [here Iowa] desired to exist in its public educational institutions." Here the Court should accord Iowa educational institutions the same right to determine for themselves to what extent free expression should be allowed in its schools as it accorded Mississippi with reference to freedom of assembly. But even if the record were silent as to protests against the Vietnam war distracting students from their assigned class work, members of this Court, like all other citizens, know, without being told, that the disputes over the wisdom of the Vietnam war have disrupted and divided this country as few other issues ever have. Of course students, like other people, cannot concentrate on lesser issues when black armbands are being ostentatiously displayed in their presence to call attention to the wounded and dead of the war, some of the wounded and the dead being their friends and neighbors. It was, of course, to distract the attention of other students that some students insisted up to the very point of their own suspension from school that they were determined to sit in school with their symbolic armbands.

Immature Students Will Soon Believe It Is Their Right to Control the Schools

Change has been said to be truly the law of life but sometimes the old and the tried and true are worth holding. The schools of this Nation have undoubtedly contributed to giving us tranquility and to making us a more law-abiding people. Uncontrolled and uncontrollable liberty is an enemy to domestic peace. We cannot close our eyes to the fact that some of the country's greatest problems are crimes committed by the youth, too many of school age. School discipline, like parental discipline, is an integral and important part of training our children to be good citizens - to be better citizens. Here a very small number of students have crisply and summarily refused to obey a school order designed to give pupils who want to learn the opportunity to do so. One does not need to be a prophet or the son of a prophet to know that after the Court's holding today some students in Iowa schools and indeed in all schools will be ready, able, and willing to defy their teachers on practically all orders.

This is the more unfortunate for the schools since groups of students all over the land are already running loose, conducting break-ins, sit-ins, lie-ins, and smash-ins. Many of these student groups, as is all too familiar to all who read the newspapers and watch the television news programs, have already engaged in rioting, property seizures, and destruction. They have picketed schools to force students not to cross their picket lines and have too often violently attacked earnest but frightened students who wanted an education that the pickets did not want them to get. Students engaged in such activities are apparently confident that they know far more about how to operate public school systems than do their parents, teachers, and elected school officials. It is no answer to say that the particular students here have not yet reached such high points in their demands to attend classes in order to exercise their political pressures. Turned loose with lawsuits for damages and injunctions against their teachers as they are here, it is nothing but wishful thinking to imagine that young, immature students will not soon believe it is their right to control the schools rather than the right of the States that collect the taxes to hire the teachers for the benefit of the pupils. This case, therefore, wholly without constitutional reasons in my judgment, subjects all the public schools in the country to the whims and caprices of their loudest-mouthed, but maybe not their brightest, students. I, for one, am not fully persuaded that school pupils are wise enough, even with this Court's expert help from Washington, to run the 23,390 public school systems in our 50 States. I wish, therefore, wholly to disclaim any purpose on my part to hold that the Federal Constitution compels the teachers, parents, and elected school officials to surrender control of the American public school system to public school students. I dissent.

"In states where the courts have been most supportive of student rights against school authority, "students reported that school discipline was both less strict and less fair."

The Court's Decision Led to the Destruction of School Discipline

Stuart Taylor Jr.

Stuart Taylor Jr. is a National Journal *columnist. In this viewpoint he discusses a book written by Richard Arum, who was formerly a high school teacher but is now a professor at New York University. Arum argues that Supreme Court decisions—beginning with* Tinker v. Des Moines, *in which the Court upheld the right of students to wear black armbands to protest the Vietnam War—are responsible for undermining the authority of schools and causing teachers to condone disruptive conduct rather than risk legal battles. Furthermore, backlash against disorderly schools has led to zero-tolerance policies that make it impossible for school officials to use common sense. Taylor points out that Justice Hugo Black's dissenting opinion in* Tinker, *warning that the ruling would subject schools to the whims of their loudest-mouthed students, now seems to have been prophetic.*

Outside Anacostia Senior High School, three miles southeast of the Capitol, a football player was killed on October 30 [2003] by a stray bullet meant for someone else. Not

Stuart Taylor, Jr., "How Courts and Congress Wrecked School Discipline," *National Journal*, vol. 35, November 15, 2003, pp. 3473–74. Copyright © 2007 by National Journal Group, Inc. All rights reserved. Reprinted with permission from National Journal.

far away, at Ballou Senior High, a gang fight involving 15 or 20 students broke out in the cafeteria on November 10. School officials "have no control," one Ballou mother complained to *The Washington Post*.

Indeed. That is the main reason why so little learning takes place at Anacostia, a part-time teacher there tells me. And nationwide, every year, some 30 students die of homicides committed on public school grounds; 10 percent of all teachers are physically threatened by students; and 4 percent are physically attacked. Student disruption of classes and defiance of teachers is routine at many schools. And such disorder is not confined to urban schools. Discipline is the biggest worry for suburban parents, too, surveys show. More than 40 percent of teachers nationwide agreed in one survey that "student behavior interferes with my teaching." Many complain that administrators don't back them up on discipline. Some leave the profession in frustration. Cheating is rampant almost everywhere, and serious punishment rare.

An idealistic young English teacher named Richard Arum began studying the breakdown in school discipline sometime after one of his students was shot three times in 1991, in the courtyard next to his classroom at Castlemont High School, in East Oakland, Calif. Arum had been drawn to the overwhelmingly black school by sympathy for the civil-rights struggle.

Now an associate professor of sociology and education at New York University, Arum has produced a new book [*Judging School Discipline*] that lays much of the responsibility at the doors of the Supreme Court, of other judges who thought they understood education better than the educators, and of the idealistic "liberal advocacy lawyers" who pushed for students' rights to challenge school discipline beginning in the 1960s. Such well-intentioned "adversarial legalism" has, Arum writes, led to "the intimidation of school personnel faced with an ambiguous legal terrain, and an undermining of the school's moral authority," all to the detriment of "the ability of public schools to socialize youth for productive roles in society." These baleful trends were not "an inevitable byproduct of change in cultural mores" or demographics, Arum adds in *Judging School Discipline*. Rather, "liberal public school advocates" must face the reality that liberal judicial decisions unique to the United States have made our schools uniquely disorderly.

Consequences of *Tinker* Were Profound

First came *Tinker v. Des Moines School District*, in 1969, in which the Supreme Court upheld public school students' First Amendment rights to wear black armbands at school to protest the Vietnam War. The justices understandably saw the suspension of these students as an overreaction. But the justices displayed their grandiosity when they suggested that telling students to do their protesting elsewhere would make the schools "enclaves of totalitarianism."

Then came *Goss v. Lopez*, in 1975, which ruled in favor of (among others) students suspended for a few days for brawling in a school lunchroom and for attacking a police officer in a school auditorium, in Columbus, Ohio. All public school students have constitutional rights not to be suspended even for a single day without notice and a due process hearing, the justices held.

However reasonable *Tinker* might seem on its facts, and however informal might be the due process hearings demanded by *Goss*, the consequences have been far more profound than allowing some sartorial protests and requiring some hearings. They have inspired hundreds of lawsuits attacking schools' authority over hair length, grades, dances, student-body elections, school newspapers, alcohol, drugs, violence, and weapons. And even though subsequent Supreme Court decisions sought to set limits to students' litigiousness—by upholding corporal punishment, for example—the genie was out of the bottle.

What's a principal to do if a gang of skinheads shows up wearing swastikas or T-shirts emblazoned with "WHITE POWER"? Are swastikas analogous to black armbands? Are shaved heads protected by precedents upholding students' rights to wear their hair long? "The principal wants to send the kid home to change, but he's not sure it's within his authority to do so, so he calls the superintendent," wrote Kay S. Hymowitz in *City Journal*. "The superintendent is also unsure, so he calls the district's lawyer. The lawyer's concern, though, isn't that the child has breached the boundaries of respect and tolerance, and needs an adult to tell him so, but whether disciplining the student would violate the First Amendment. Is this, in other words, literally a federal case?"

This legal uncertainty, which clouds every disciplinary decision with doubt and clogs educational systems with complex due process administrative rules, is only the tip of an iceberg of social instability. As consensus over once-unquestioned moral norms has broken down, judicial decisions have, for many, become the default source of moral instruction. So when the Supreme Court gives violent or disruptive students the constitutional right to sue their schools, it also gives them a sense of empowerment against all authority and saddles teachers and administrators with "hesitation, doubt, and weakening of conviction," in Arum's words.

Right vs. Wrong Replaced by Legalisms

"The mere potential for a lawsuit shrinks the adult in the child's eyes," as Hymowitz puts it. "The natural relationship between adult and child begins to crumble." Educators "hesitate to assert the most basic civic and moral values that might pose a challenge to the crude and status-crazed peer culture." And the language of right and wrong gives way to the language of legalisms, interspersed with therapeutic psychobabble.

Even when disciplinary decisions are upheld, the hearing process grinds down school officials and makes them gun-shy. "I've been named now three times in lawsuits," one principal recalled in a recent Public Agenda survey. "You go to these depositions and they'll ask you about a conversation I had three years ago in the hallway. 'Who was there? Who else heard? What exactly did you say? Did you keep any notes?' I think it's devastating."

Since the best defense to a complaint by an angry student or parent is rigorous compliance with "due process," teachers focus on documenting their reasons for even the mildest discipline of the worst actors, rather than on how best to teach the students who want to learn. And many teachers and administrators take the path of least resistance by condoning disruptive conduct rather than risking legal battles. One teacher told Public Agenda that he has become hesitant to break up student fights. In the old days, he said, "I was thinking about the kids," and about preventing injury. Now, he's "more thinking of litigation."

School Discipline Has Become Less Fair

Has all this made school discipline more fair? No. Comparative analysis shows, according to Arum, that in states where the courts have been most supportive of student rights against school authority, "students reported that school discipline was both less strict and less fair."

Congress has also done much damage, beginning with its adoption in 1975 of the law now known as the Individuals with Disabilities Education Act. While justifiably vindicating the rights of wheelchair-bound and other disabled kids (including a onetime client of mine) to free public education, that law has also made it impossible to expel, and extremely difficult to discipline, any student diagnosed as having "serious emotional disturbance"—a concept broad enough to include just about any chronically disruptive child. Even kids who have sexually assaulted their teachers have been returned to their classrooms.

What is to be done? The mindless "zero-tolerance" policies produced by the backlash against disorderly schools have only made matters worse, by further undermining school officials' discretion to use their common sense. Take the case of the 6-year-old who brought a pocketknife that her grandpa had given her to school in response to her teacher's suggestion that kids bring something special that they cherished. "I had to suspend her for several days," a rueful administrator told Public Agenda.

Arum asserts that giving school officials completely unchecked power over students is not the answer. It is for the courts to make clear that they will intervene to ensure fairness only in "situations involving long-term exclusion or suppression of student First Amendment rights."

But it will not be easy to undo the damage. In a dissenting opinion, Justice Hugo Black warned that *Tinker* would subject "all the public schools in the country to the whims and caprices of their loudest-mouthed, but maybe not their brightest, students." At the time, it appeared to many that the great civil libertarian had become an old fuddy-duddy. Now he seems more like a prophet.

"If recent evidence is correct, all too many high school students don't understand their First Amendment rights."

The Issue of Free Speech for Students Is Still Current

Mark Walsh

Mark Walsh is an assistant editor of Education Week. *In the following selection he tells what has since happened to John and Mary Beth Tinker, who in 1965 wore armbands to school to protest the Vietnam War and whose case resulted in the Supreme Court's establishment of student rights to free speech. Now, as adults, they visit schools to talk to today's students. They are often asked whether the Court's decision would be different if the case were heard today. Mary Beth Tinker thinks it might be, and some experts agree, because threats to schools have changed. Others, including John Tinker, believe that the case has become so important in school law that it would be difficult to overturn.*

Forty years after they stood up for their right to wear anti-war armbands, Mary Beth and John Tinker advise students that free speech is still worth fighting for.

John and Mary Beth Tinker are back in a classroom in their hometown, once again wearing black armbands and drawing attention to a war.

Now in their 50s, the siblings are living symbols of constitutional rights for secondary school students. In 1965, they and a handful of others were suspended for wearing black

Mark Walsh, "Living History," *Education Week*, vol. 24, May 4, 2005. Reproduced by permission.

armbands to their public schools here to protest the Vietnam War. The Tinkers and another student, Christopher Eckhardt, took their case all the way to the U.S. Supreme Court, where in 1969 they won the landmark ruling in *Tinker v. Des Moines Independent Community School District* that wearing such an armband in school was symbolic speech protected by the First Amendment as long as school was not substantially disrupted.

"All of us are concerned about the war in Iraq," Mary Beth tells a group of about 90 middle and high school students at Central Academy, a public magnet school where students take Advanced Placement courses and other specialized offerings.

Her brother is more direct. "We're in the middle of a war that many, many people think is illegal," he says about the U.S. military operation in Iraq. He will say several times in four public appearances over two days in Iowa last month that while Saddam Hussein was "a bad guy," the war is all about controlling resources such as oil.

John is soft-spoken and almost apologizes to the Central Academy students for hitting them with such contentious issues as the war, the Patriot Act, and the continuing influence of "the military-industrial complex." "I don't want to step on anyone's toes, politically," he says. "We started out as peace activists before we became First Amendment activists."

Advocates for Student Expression

Today, nearly 40 years after the armband controversy unfolded, the Tinkers tend carefully to their legacy as advocates for student expression. They often crisscross the country to speak at schools. John, 54, happily answers e-mail queries from students of all ages, even when they have neglected to do the most basic background reading about the case. Mary Beth, 52, sometimes writes privately to lend encouragement to students embroiled in free-speech disputes in their schools.

Many students of this generation who study their case feel awestruck when they encounter the Tinkers in person. "I idolize them," says Thomas Clough, 18, a senior who was at the Central Academy event in April. "They were willing to stand up for what they believed in."

Michael Schaffer, the AP government teacher at Central Academy, introduced the Tinkers as "two American heroes. These are people who made a difference."

Later, he says that his classes, which draw students from every Des Moines high school and from suburban districts, are full of students "who would be the present-day Tinkers. These are students who would be committed to taking a stand on principle," he says.

But if recent evidence is correct, all too many high school students don't understand their First Amendment rights. A survey of 112,000 students released this year by the John S. and James L. Knight Foundation found that a majority were apathetic about, or ignorant of, those rights. More than a third thought the amendment's guarantees went too far. . . .

Looking Back

In the fall of 1965, John was a 15-year-old sophomore at North High School in Des Moines, where he played in the band and hung out with the chess players. "I had plenty of friends, but I did tend to hang out with the nonconformists," he says.

Mary Beth was a 13-year-old 8th grader at Warren Harding Junior High School who was interested in roller skating and pizza parties. But she was also paying more and more attention to the escalating U.S. involvement in Vietnam. "I just remember coming home and watching the war on TV and feeling real bad about it," she says.

That fall, the Tinkers' local morning newspaper, the *Des Moines Register*, carried headlines almost daily about the deepening war. Over Thanksgiving weekend of 1965, John Tinker, Chris Eckhardt, and Margaret Eckhardt, Chris' mother and a local peace activist, rode buses to Washington to join 25,000 others for one of the first big marches against the U.S. military commitment.

On the bus ride home, an energized group of Iowans discussed what they might do next. Someone suggested the wearing of black armbands, and when the group returned to Des Moines, numerous students met at the Eckhardts' home and agreed on a plan to wear armbands to school on Dec. 16 to mourn the dead in Vietnam and support Sen. Robert F. Kennedy's call for a Christmas truce.

School administrators in the Des Moines district, which then had about 18,000 students, got wind of the plan and met to respond. The district's five high school principals decided to prohibit the wearing of armbands in school, word of which made it onto the front page of the *Register* on Dec. 15. Accounts vary as to how many students wore armbands to school, but John Tinker says it was at least a dozen. Seven students were suspended, including the three who would be at the center of the legal challenge: Chris Eckhardt and John and Mary Beth Tinker.

Mary Beth wore her armband on the sleeve of her sweater Dec. 16. While she drew attention and whispers from classmates, she did not face any problems until she reached her math class in the early afternoon. Her teacher, Richard Moberly, had held a discussion the previous day about protests and strongly suggested that no one wear an armband to his class. Mary Beth was sent to the school office, where, she points out to students today, she felt so intimidated she actually removed her armband. But she was suspended anyway.

John Tinker did not wear his armband until the next day. He wore a coat and tie, which was dressier than the norm but not highly unusual in that less-casual era for school attire. "I wanted to keep the issue on the armband," John says. "I wanted to exhibit respect generally."

But when John pinned his armband on over his dark jacket, it wasn't very noticeable. Only at midday, after he had changed out of his gym clothes, did he decide to wear the armband over his crisp white dress shirt. Then it got noticed.

John's principal at North High told him that being disciplined for wearing an armband would look bad on his permanent record, and that a more appropriate way to mourn the war dead would be to take part in a Memorial Day ceremony.

After several weeks of debate, the Des Moines school board upheld the administrative ban on armbands. Meanwhile, the Christmas break had brought a cooling-off period. The students agreed to return to school in January 1966 without armbands. But John and Mary Beth continued their protest another way: They wore all-black clothing for the rest of the year. John says he discarded the armband he wore to school at some point. Mary Beth saved hers and intends to donate it to a new First Amendment museum being planned in Chicago. . . .

The Tinkers' Adult Lives

By 1969, the Tinkers had moved to St. Louis, and Mary Beth was adjusting to life in a new high school. She remembers *Time* magazine shooting photos in her chemistry class when she would rather have just blended into the crowd.

Mary Beth shunned higher education at first, working to repair and tune pianos. She eventually became a nurse, and went to work for several years for the Veterans Administration. She now works as a nurse in the pediatric unit of a Los Angeles hospital. "As a nurse, I work with kids a lot," she says. "I know kids need to have self-expression. It strengthens their core personality and ability to speak out later."

She has a son, who now attends Princeton University. When he was in the 6th grade, he got in trouble at school for throwing an eraser at the chalkboard. When Mary Beth came to school for a conference, the principal told her that her son had said: "Have you ever heard of the *Tinker* case? That's my mom." The principal told the boy: "That's not going to help you today."

John Tinker was attending the University of Iowa when the case reached the Supreme Court. He missed the oral arguments in Washington because he fell asleep in the airport and failed to catch his flight. He later dropped out of college and obtained conscientious-objector status in the military draft. "I had become convinced that academia was not the answer," he says. "If academia were the answer, the problem would already be solved."

He moved to Corpus Christi, Texas, where his maternal grandparents lived, and went to work on a shrimp boat. He remembers trying to further educate himself by reading quotation books cover to cover. "In quotation books, you're getting the condensed values of the culture," he says.

Eventually, he learned about computers, and even joined the "cubicle culture" by going to work as a systems analyst for MCI. But he also kept his interest in liberal causes. He ran a program called Peace Parts, which brought leftover electronics components to Nicaragua. . . .

Mary Beth says that for many years, she shied away from speaking about the case. She traces her reluctance to threats her family received during the height of the armband protest. She eventually convinced herself that speaking about the case, especially to young audiences, would encourage more individuals to stand up for their rights.

Jamin B. Raskin, a law professor at American University in Washington and the author of a book about students' rights, has brought Mary Beth to the nation's capital numerous times to speak to students.

"She's like a rock star when we take her out to schools," he says. "She is not a person who is frozen in time. She continues to be passionate in her politics and daring in her speech.". . .

Times Have Changed

On this trip to Iowa, preceding their visit to Central Academy, John and Mary Beth Tinker have traveled about 45 minutes north of Des Moines to Iowa State University in Ames.

Joining college students in the audience of nearly 200 people are a handful of 8th graders from Akron-Westfield Middle School in Akron, Iowa. They have driven four hours to be here to meet the Tinkers, and they have to drive back the same night.

"There is no topic that has gotten our students excited like this," says teacher Val Philips. The students have selected the *Tinker* case for a dramatic performance as their entry in a National History Day competition. They have been e-mailing John for details about the case, and he has obliged. After the event, the students crowd around the siblings and ask for their autographs, with one 8th grader telling Mary Beth: "We've been counting down the days and hours."

"We picked *Tinker v. Des Moines* because we didn't know that much about it at first," says Becca Meerdink, 14. "We didn't really know we had our rights."

At the Iowa State forum, the Tinkers are asked a question they often get: What would happen if their case came before the Supreme Court today?

Mary Beth says, "I'd think we'd lose, but I don't know."

Some scholars agree. John W. Johnson, a history professor at the University of Northern Iowa and the author of *The Struggle for Student Rights*, a 1997 book about the armband case, says the current Supreme Court would view the case through the lens of the 1999 Columbine High School shootings. "Times have changed," Johnson says. "Threats to schools have changed. If this case were up in this term of the Supreme Court, it would go the other way."

But Raskin of American University says that while "there has been a lot of bad news on the Supreme Court for student rights in the last couple of decades," the *Tinker* decision "has achieved a kind of sacrosanct status in our law."

John Tinker shares that view. "For the court to reverse this decision," he says, "they would really have a lot of explaining to do."

CHAPTER 2

Denying Free Speech in Official School Publications

Case Overview

Hazelwood School District
v. Kuhlmeier (1988)

When the principal of Hazelwood East High School deleted several pages of stories from the school newspaper, its student editors were upset. They felt their right to free speech had been violated, so with the encouragement of their former teacher, they took the case to court. When they lost in the District Court, their attorney appealed to the Circuit Court, which reversed the lower court's decision, and the school board then appealed to the U.S. Supreme Court.

The principal, Robert Reynolds, had believed that two stories in the paper were inappropriate—one of them, about student pregnancy, because he thought the girls it dealt with might be identifiable despite the fact that their names were not given; the other, about the effect of divorce, because the parents criticized by a student had not been given a chance to respond. (He was unaware that the name of that student, too, had been deleted from the final draft.) He also thought that the subject of teen pregnancy was unsuitable for the younger students who would read the paper. Believing that there was not enough time to make changes before the deadline, he deleted not just the two stories but the entire pages on which they appeared.

The case hinged on whether the school newspaper should be considered a public forum. The Circuit Court said that it should, but the Supreme Court disagreed. It pointed out that the paper was produced during regular class hours as part of the school curriculum, and that the journalism teacher exercised control over it by choosing the editors and making story assignments. Therefore, there was no evidence that the school meant it to be anything more than a supervised learning experience for students enrolled in journalism, and the constitutional right to free speech that exists in public forums was not applicable to its staff. The Court went on to rule that schools can censor any school-sponsored expressive activity, as distinguished from the personal expressions of students, as long as there is a reasonable educational reason for doing so.

This was an unpopular decision. Only five of the nine justices of the Supreme Court concurred in it. Three others joined in a dissenting opinion, in which they stated that they did not believe a distinction should be made between personal and school-sponsored speech; that the Court should not have departed from the standard set by *Tinker v. Des Moines*; and that disclaimers could eliminate the problem of having student views attributed to the school administration. Because journalists tend to oppose all forms of censorship, media coverage of the ruling was largely unfavorable. Not many people other than school officials seemed impressed by the argument that a publisher—in this case, the school—generally does have some say about what is published, although it was recognized that students do still have the right to print whatever they want in underground papers not sponsored by the school.

The precedent set by *Hazelwood v. Kuhlmeier* is seen as a major modification of the *Tinker* standard and has had impact far beyond school newspapers. Schools have exerted more control than they did previously over everything from mascots to graduation ceremonies, and federal courts have usually backed them up. Part of the reason for the increase in court cases, however, may be that high school students have become more assertive and have opposed school policies more often than did earlier generations. As Mike Hiestand, an attorney for the Student Press Law Center has pointed out, "They're not just writing about football games and proms anymore."

"The standard articulated in Tinker *for determining when a school may punish student expression need not also be the standard for determining when a school may refuse to lend its name and resources to the dissemination of student expression."*

The Court's Decision: A School Need Not Disseminate Student Speech Inconsistent with Its Basic Educational Mission

Byron White

Byron White, who was a star professional football player before he became an attorney, was a justice of the U.S. Supreme Court from 1962 until 1993. He generally took a broad view of governmental powers and opposed placing restrictions on the police; for instance, he dissented in the landmark case of Miranda v. Arizona, *in which the Court ruled that all criminal defendants must be read their rights at the time of arrest. He also dissented in* Roe v. Wade, *which established women's rights to abortion. The following selection is the opinion he delivered in the case of* Hazelwood School District v. Kuhlmeier. *In it he explains why the principal of Hazelwood East High School censored articles in the school newspaper and concludes that he acted reasonably in doing so. A school newspaper is not a public forum, Justice White says, and a school need not promote speech inconsistent*

Byron White, majority opinion, *Hazelwood School District et al. v. Kuhlmeier et al.*, U.S. Supreme Court, January 13, 1988.

with its basic educational mission in an activity that is part of the school curriculum. This is a different issue from the issue in Tinker v. Des Moines, which involved suppression of students' personal expressions on school premises, and therefore that precedent does not apply. Thus, Justice White says, there was no violation of the First Amendment in this case.

The practice at Hazelwood East during the spring 1983 semester was for the journalism teacher to submit page proofs of each *Spectrum* issue to Principal Reynolds for his review prior to publication. On May 10, Emerson delivered the proofs of the May 13 edition to Reynolds, who objected to two of the articles scheduled to appear in that edition. One of the stories described three Hazelwood East students' experiences with pregnancy; the other discussed the impact of divorce on students at the school.

Reynolds was concerned that, although the pregnancy story used false names "to keep the identity of these girls a secret," the pregnant students still might be identifiable from the text. He also believed that the article's references to sexual activity and birth control were inappropriate for some of the younger students at the school. In addition, Reynolds was concerned that a student identified by name in the divorce story had complained that her father "wasn't spending enough time with my mom, my sister and I" prior to the divorce, "was always out of town on business or out late playing cards with the guys," and "always argued about everything" with her mother. Reynolds believed that the student's parents should have been given an opportunity to respond to these remarks or to consent to their publication. He was unaware that Emerson had deleted the student's name from the final version of the article.

Reynolds believed that there was no time to make the necessary changes in the stories before the scheduled press run and that the newspaper would not appear before the end of the school year if printing were delayed to any significant extent. He concluded that his only options under the circumstances were to publish a four-page newspaper instead of the planned six-page newspaper, eliminating the two pages on which the offending stories appeared, or to publish no newspaper at all. Accordingly, he directed Emerson to withhold from publication the two pages containing the stories on pregnancy and divorce. He informed his superiors of the decision, and they concurred.

District Court and Circuit Court Decisions

Respondents subsequently commenced this action in the United States District Court for the Eastern District of Missouri seeking a declaration that their First Amendment rights had been violated, injunctive relief, and monetary damages. After a bench trial, the District Court denied an injunction, holding that no First Amendment violation had occurred. . . .

The court found that Principal Reynolds' concern that the pregnant students' anonymity would be lost and their privacy invaded was "legitimate and reasonable," given "the small number of pregnant students at Hazelwood East and several identifying characteristics that were disclosed in the article." The court held that Reynolds' action was also justified "to avoid the impression that [the school] endorses the sexual norms of the subjects" and to shield younger students from exposure to unsuitable material. The deletion of the article on divorce was seen by the court as a reasonable response to the invasion of privacy concerns raised by the named student's remarks. Because the article did not indicate that the student's parents had been offered an opportunity to respond to her allegations, said the court, there was cause for "serious doubt that the article complied with the rules of fairness which are standard in the field of journalism and which were covered in the textbook used in the Journalism II class." Furthermore, the court concluded that Reynolds was justified in deleting two full pages of the newspaper, instead of deleting only the pregnancy and divorce stories or requiring that those stories be modified to address his concerns, based on his "reasonable belief that he had to make an immediate decision and that there was no time to make modifications to the articles in question."

The Court of Appeals for the Eighth Circuit reversed. The court held at the outset that *Spectrum* was not only "a part of the school adopted curriculum," but also a public forum, because the newspaper was "intended to be and operated as a conduit for student viewpoint." The court then concluded that *Spectrum*'s status as a public forum precluded school officials from censoring its contents except when "'necessary to avoid material and substantial interference with school work or discipline . . . or the rights of others.'" Id., at 1374 (quoting *Tinker v. Des Moines Independent Community School Dist.*).

The Court of Appeals found "no evidence in the record that the principal could have reasonably forecast that the censored articles or any materials in the censored articles would have materially disrupted classwork or given rise to substantial disorder in the school." School officials were entitled to censor the articles on the ground that they invaded the rights of others, according to the court, only if publication of the articles could have resulted in tort liability to the school. The court concluded that no tort action for libel or invasion of privacy could have been maintained against the school by the subjects of the two articles or by their families. Accordingly, the court held that school officials had violated respondents' First Amendment rights by deleting the two pages of the newspaper.

We granted certiorari, and we now reverse.

Rights of Students in School Are Not the Same as Those of Adults

Students in the public schools do not "shed their constitutional rights to freedom of speech or expression at the schoolhouse gate." *Tinker*. They cannot be punished merely for expressing their personal views on the school premises—whether "in the cafeteria, or on the playing field, or on the campus during the authorized hours,"—unless school authorities have reason to believe that such expression will "substantially interfere with the work of the school or impinge upon the rights of other students."

We have nonetheless recognized that the First Amendment rights of students in the public schools "are not automatically coextensive with the rights of adults in other settings," *Bethel School District No. 403 v. Fraser*, and must be "applied in light of the special characteristics of the school environment." *Tinker*. A school need not tolerate student speech that is inconsistent with its "basic educational mission," *Fraser*, even though the government could not censor similar speech outside the school. Accordingly, we held in *Fraser* that a student could be disciplined for having delivered a speech that was "sexually explicit" but not legally obscene at an official school assembly, because the school was entitled to "disassociate itself" from the speech in a manner that would demonstrate to others that such vulgarity is "wholly inconsistent with the 'fundamental values' of public school education." We thus recognized that "[t]he determination of what manner of speech in the classroom or in school assembly is inappropriate properly rests with the school board," rather than with the federal courts. It is in this context that respondents' First Amendment claims must be considered.

Was the School Newspaper a Public Forum?

We deal first with the question whether *Spectrum* may appropriately be characterized as a forum for public expression. The public schools do not possess all of the attributes of streets, parks, and other traditional public forums that "time out of mind, have been used for purposes of assembly, communicating thoughts between citizens, and discussing public questions." *Hague v. CIO.* Hence, school facilities may be deemed to be public forums only if school authorities have "by policy or by practice" opened those facilities "for indiscriminate use by the general public," *Perry Education Assn. v. Perry Local Educators' Assn.*, or by some segment of the public, such as student organizations. If the facilities have instead been reserved for other intended purposes, "communicative or otherwise," then no public forum has been created, and school officials may impose reasonable restrictions on the speech of students, teachers, and other members of the school community. . . .

The Hazelwood East Curriculum Guide described the Journalism II course as a "laboratory situation in which the students publish the school newspaper applying skills they have learned in Journalism I." The lessons that were to be learned from the Journalism II course, according to the Curriculum Guide, included development of journalistic skills under deadline pressure, "the legal, moral, and ethical restrictions imposed upon journalists within the school community," and "responsibility and acceptance of criticism for articles of opinion." Journalism II was taught by a faculty member during regular class hours. Students received grades and academic credit for their performance in the course. . . .

The District Court found that Robert Stergos, the journalism teacher during most of the 1982–1983 school year, "both had the authority to exercise and in fact exercised a great deal of control over *Spectrum*." For example, Stergos selected the editors of the newspaper, scheduled publication dates, decided the number of pages for each issue, assigned story ideas to class members, advised students on the development of their stories, reviewed the use of quotations, edited stories, selected and edited the letters to the editor, and dealt with the printing company. Many of these decisions were made without consultation with the Journalism II students. The District Court thus found it "clear that Mr. Stergos was the final authority with respect to almost every aspect of the production and publication of *Spectrum*, including its content." Moreover, after each Spectrum issue had been finally approved by Stergos or his successor, the issue still had to be reviewed by Principal Reynolds prior to publication. Respondents' assertion that they had believed that they could publish "practically anything" in *Spectrum* was therefore dismissed by the District Court as simply "not credible."...

The evidence relied upon by the Court of Appeals in finding *Spectrum* to be a public forum, is equivocal at best.... That students were permitted to exercise some authority over the contents of *Spectrum* was fully consistent with the Curriculum Guide objective of teaching the Journalism II students "leadership responsibilities as issue and page editors." App. 11. A decision to teach leadership skills in the context of a classroom activity hardly implies a decision to relinquish school control over that activity. In sum, the evidence relied upon by the Court of Appeals fails to demonstrate the "clear intent to create a public forum," *Cornelius*, that existed in cases in which we found public forums to have been created. School officials did not evince either "by policy or by practice," *Perry Education Assn.*, any intent to open the pages of *Spectrum* to "indiscriminate use," ibid., by its student reporters and editors, or by the student body generally. Instead, they "reserve[d] the forum for its intended purpos[e]," as a supervised learning experience for journalism students. Accordingly, school officials were entitled to regulate the contents of *Spectrum* in any reasonable manner. It is this standard, rather than our decision in *Tinker*, that governs this case.

The Issue in *Tinker* Is Different from the Issue in This Case

The question whether the First Amendment requires a school to tolerate particular student speech—the question that we addressed in *Tinker*—is different from the question whether the First Amendment requires a school affirmatively to promote particular student speech. The former question addresses educators' ability to silence a student's personal expression that happens to occur on the school premises. The latter question concerns educators' authority over school-sponsored publications, theatrical productions, and other expressive activities that students, parents, and members of the public might reasonably perceive to bear the imprimatur of the school. These activities may fairly be characterized as part of the school curriculum, whether or not they occur in a traditional classroom setting, so long as they are supervised by faculty members and designed to impart particular knowledge or skills to student participants and audiences.

Educators are entitled to exercise greater control over this second form of student expression to assure that participants learn whatever lessons the activity is designed to teach, that readers or listeners are not exposed to material that may be inappropriate for their level of maturity, and that the views of the individual speaker are not erroneously attributed to the school. Hence, a school may in its capacity as publisher of a school newspaper or producer of a school play "disassociate itself," *Fraser*, not only from speech that would "substantially interfere with [its] work . . . or impinge upon the rights of other students," *Tinker*, but also from speech that is, for example, ungrammatical, poorly written, inadequately researched, biased or prejudiced, vulgar or profane, or unsuitable for immature audiences. A school must be able to set high standards for the student speech that is disseminated under its auspices—standards that may be higher than those demanded by some newspaper publishers or theatrical producers in the "real" world—and may refuse to disseminate student speech that does not meet those standards. In addition, a school must be able to take into account the emotional maturity of the intended audience in determining whether to disseminate student speech on potentially sensitive topics, which might range from the existence of Santa Claus in an elementary school setting to the particulars of teenage sexual activity in a high school setting. A school must also retain the authority to refuse to sponsor student speech that might reasonably be perceived to advocate drug or alcohol use, irresponsible sex, or conduct otherwise inconsistent with "the shared values of a civilized social order," *Fraser*, or to associate the school with any position other than neutrality on matters of political controversy. Otherwise, the schools would be unduly constrained from fulfilling their role as "a principal instrument in awakening the child to cultural values, in preparing him for later professional training, and in helping him to adjust normally to his environment." *Brown v. Board of Education.*

Accordingly, we conclude that the standard articulated in *Tinker* for determining when a school may punish student expression need not also be the standard for determining when a school may refuse to lend its name and resources to the dissemination of student expression. Instead, we hold that educators do not offend the First Amendment by exercising editorial control over the style and content of student speech in school-sponsored expressive activities so long as their actions are reasonably related to legitimate pedagogical concerns.

This standard is consistent with our oft-expressed view that the education of the Nation's youth is primarily the responsibility of parents, teachers, and state and local school officials, and not of federal judges. It is only when the decision to censor a school-sponsored publication, theatrical production, or other vehicle of student expression has no valid educational purpose that the First Amendment is so "directly and sharply implicate[d]," ibid., as to require judicial intervention to protect students' constitutional rights.

The Principal Acted Reasonably

We also conclude that Principal Reynolds acted reasonably in requiring the deletion from the May 13 issue of *Spectrum* of the pregnancy article, the divorce article, and the remaining articles that were to appear on the same pages of the newspaper.

The initial paragraph of the pregnancy article declared that "[a]ll names have been changed to keep the identity of these girls a secret." The principal concluded that the students' anonymity was not adequately protected, however, given the other identifying information in the article and the small number of pregnant students at the school. Reynolds therefore could reasonably have feared that the article violated whatever pledge of anonymity had been given to the pregnant students. In addition, he could reasonably have been concerned that the article was not sufficiently sensitive to the privacy interests of the students' boyfriends and parents, who were discussed in the article but who were given no opportunity to consent to its publication or to offer a response. . . .

The student who was quoted by name in the version of the divorce article seen by Principal Reynolds made comments sharply critical of her father. The principal could reasonably have concluded that an individual publicly identified as an inattentive parent—indeed, as one who chose "playing cards with the guys" over home and family—was entitled to an opportunity to defend himself as a matter of journalistic fairness. These concerns were shared by both of *Spectrum*'s faculty advisers for the 1982–1983 school year, who testified that they would not have allowed the article to be printed without deletion of the student's name.

Principal Reynolds testified credibly at trial that, at the time that he reviewed the proofs of the May 13 issue during an extended telephone conversation with Emerson, he believed that there was no time to make any changes in the articles, and that the newspaper had to be printed immediately or not at all. . . .

Reynolds could reasonably have concluded that the students who had written and edited these articles had not sufficiently mastered those portions of the Journalism II curriculum that pertained to the treatment of controversial issues and personal attacks, the need to protect the privacy of individuals whose most intimate concerns are to be revealed in the newspaper, and "the legal, moral, and ethical restrictions imposed upon journalists within [a] school community" that includes adolescent subjects and readers. Finally, we conclude that the principal's decision to delete two pages of *Spectrum*, rather than to delete only the offending articles or to require that they be modified, was reasonable under the circumstances as he understood them. Accordingly, no violation of First Amendment rights occurred.

The judgment of the Court of Appeals for the Eighth Circuit is therefore reversed.

"The case before us aptly illustrates how readily school officials (and courts) can camouflage viewpoint discrimination as the "mere" protection of students from sensitive topics."

Dissenting Opinion: No Distinction Should Be Made Between Personal and School-Sponsored Speech

William Brennan

William Brennan was a justice of the U.S. Supreme Court from 1956 to 1990. He was an outspoken liberal especially noted for his support of civil rights and the expansion of First Amendment rights. The following viewpoint is his dissenting opinion in the case of Hazelwood School District v. Kuhlmeier, *which was joined by Justices Thurgood Marshall and Harry Blackmun. These justices disagreed with the Court's majority decision that school censorship of school-sponsored projects such as the school newspaper is permissible even though it is a violation of the First Amendment to suppress other student expression. They did not believe there was justification for making such a distinction. The one thing that might justify it—the risk that views expressed in the newspaper might be attributed to the school—could be dealt with by other means, such as publication of a disclaimer. Furthermore, Justice Brennan says, the school principal accom-*

William Brennan, dissenting opinion, *Hazelwood School District et al. v. Kuhlmeier et al.*, U.S. Supreme Court, January 13, 1988.

plished the censorship in a manner "intolerable from any state official," and the Court's ruling will therefore teach young people the wrong kind of civics lesson.

When the young men and women of Hazelwood East High School registered for Journalism II, they expected a civics lesson. *Spectrum*, the newspaper they were to publish, "was not just a class exercise in which students learned to prepare papers and hone writing skills, it was a . . . forum established to give students an opportunity to express their views while gaining an appreciation of their rights and responsibilities under the First Amendment to the United States Constitution. . . ."

The school board itself affirmatively guaranteed the students of Journalism II an atmosphere conducive to fostering such an appreciation and exercising the full panoply of rights associated with a free student press. "School sponsored student publications," it vowed, "will not restrict free expression or diverse viewpoints within the rules of responsible journalism."

This case arose when the Hazelwood East administration breached its own promise, dashing its students' expectations. The school principal, without prior consultation or explanation, excised six articles—comprising two full pages—of the May 13, 1983, issue of *Spectrum*. He did so not because any of the articles would "materially and substantially interfere with the requirements of appropriate discipline," but simply because he considered two of the six "inappropriate, personal, sensitive, and unsuitable" for student consumption.

In my view the principal broke more than just a promise. He violated the First Amendment's prohibitions against censorship of any student expression that neither disrupts classwork nor invades the rights of others, and against any censorship that is not narrowly tailored to serve its purpose. . . .

Educators Must Allow Some Student Expression That Offends Them

While the "constitutional rights of students in public school are not automatically coextensive with the rights of adults in other settings," *Fraser*, students in the public schools do not "shed their constitutional rights to freedom of speech or expression at the schoolhouse gate," *Tinker*. Just as the public on the street corner must, in the interest of fostering "enlightened opinion," *Cantwell v. Connecticut*, tolerate speech that "tempt[s] [the listener] to throw [the speaker] off the street," public educators must accommodate some student expression even if it offends them or offers views or values that contradict those the school wishes to inculcate.

In *Tinker*, this Court struck the balance. We held that official censorship of student expression—there the suspension of several students until they removed their armbands protesting the Vietnam war—is unconstitutional unless the speech "materially disrupts classwork or involves substantial disorder or invasion of the rights of others." School officials may not suppress "silent, passive expression of opinion, unaccompanied by any disorder or disturbance on the part of" the speaker. The "mere desire to avoid the discomfort and unpleasantness that always accompany an unpopular viewpoint," or an unsavory subject, does not justify official suppression of student speech in the high school.

This Court applied the *Tinker* test just a Term ago in *Fraser*, upholding an official decision to discipline a student for delivering a lewd speech in support of a student-government candidate. The Court today casts no doubt on *Tinker*'s vitality. Instead it erects a taxonomy of school censorship, concluding that *Tinker* applies to one category and not another. On the one hand is censorship "to silence a student's personal expression that happens to occur on the school premises." On the other hand is censorship of expression that arises in the context of "school-sponsored . . . expressive activities that students, parents, and members of the public might reasonably perceive to bear the imprimatur of the school."

The Court does not, for it cannot, purport to discern from our precedents the distinction it creates. One could, I suppose, readily characterize the students' symbolic speech in *Tinker* as "personal expression that happens to [have] occur[red] on school premises," although *Tinker* did not even hint that the personal nature of the speech was of any (much less dispositive) relevance. But that same description could not by any stretch of the imagination fit *Fraser*'s speech. He did not just "happen" to deliver his lewd speech to an ad hoc gathering on the playground. As the second paragraph of *Fraser* evinces, if ever a forum for student expression was "school-sponsored," *Fraser*'s was:

> "Fraser ... delivered a speech nominating a fellow student for student elective office. Approximately 600 high school students ... attended the assembly. Students were required to attend the assembly or to report to the study hall. The assembly was part of a school-sponsored educational program in self-government."

Yet, from the first sentence of its analysis, *Fraser* faithfully applied *Tinker*.

Nor has this Court ever intimated a distinction between personal and school-sponsored speech in any other context. Particularly telling is this Court's heavy reliance on *Tinker* in two cases of First Amendment infringement on state college campuses. . . .

The Excuses Do Not Support Distinction Between School-sponsored and Other Speech

Even if we were writing on a clean slate, I would reject the Court's rationale for abandoning *Tinker* in this case. The Court offers no more than an obscure tangle of three excuses to afford educators "greater control" over school-sponsored speech than the *Tinker* test would permit: the public educator's prerogative to control curriculum; the pedagogical interest in shielding the high school audience from objectionable viewpoints and sensitive topics; and the school's need to dissociate itself from student expression. None of the excuses, once disentangled, supports the distinction that the Court draws. *Tinker* fully addresses the first concern; the second is illegitimate; and the third is readily achievable through less oppressive means.

The Court is certainly correct that the First Amendment permits educators "to assure that participants learn whatever lessons the activity is designed to teach. . . ." That is, however, the essence of the *Tinker* test, not an excuse to abandon it. Under *Tinker*, school officials may censor only such student speech as would "materially disrup[t]" a legitimate curricular function. Manifestly, student speech is more likely to disrupt a curricular function when it arises in the context of a curricular activity—one that "is designed to teach" something—than when it arises in the context of a noncurricular activity. Thus, under *Tinker*, the school may constitutionally punish the budding political orator if he disrupts calculus class but not if he holds his tongue for the cafeteria. That is not because some more stringent standard applies in the curricular context. (After all, this Court applied the same standard whether the students in *Tinker* wore their armbands to the "classroom" or the "cafeteria.") It is because student speech in the noncurricular context is less likely to disrupt materially any legitimate pedagogical purpose.

I fully agree with the Court that the First Amendment should afford an educator the prerogative not to sponsor the publication of a newspaper article that is "ungrammatical, poorly written, inadequately researched, biased or prejudiced," or that falls short of the "high standards for . . . student speech that is disseminated under [the school's] auspices. . . ." But we need not abandon *Tinker* to reach that conclusion; we need only apply it. The enumerated criteria reflect the skills that the curricular newspaper "is designed to teach." The educator may, under *Tinker,* constitutionally "censor" poor grammar, writing, or research because to reward such expression would "materially disrup[t]" the newspaper's curricular purpose.

The same cannot be said of official censorship designed to shield the audience or dissociate the sponsor from the expression. Censorship so motivated might well serve (although, as I demonstrate, cannot legitimately serve) some other school purpose. But it in no way furthers the curricular purposes of a student newspaper, unless one believes that the purpose of the school newspaper is to teach students that the press ought never report bad news, express unpopular views, or print a thought that might upset its sponsors. Unsurprisingly, Hazelwood East claims no such pedagogical purpose.

The Principal's Action Was Not a Lesson in Journalism

The Court relies on bits of testimony to portray the principal's conduct as a pedagogical lesson to Journalism II students who "had not sufficiently mastered those portions of the . . . curriculum that pertained to the treatment of controversial issues and personal attacks, the need to protect the privacy of individuals . . . , and 'the legal, moral, and ethical restrictions imposed upon journalists. . . .'"

But the principal never consulted the students before censoring their work. "[T]hey learned of the deletions when the paper was released." Further, he explained the deletions only in the broadest of generalities. In one meeting called at the behest of seven protesting *Spectrum* staff members (presumably a fraction of the full class), he characterized the articles as "'too sensitive' for 'our immature audience of readers,'" and in a later meeting he deemed them simply "inappropriate, personal, sensitive and unsuitable for the newspaper." The Court's supposition that the principal intended (or the protesters understood) those generalities as a lesson on the nuances of journalistic responsibility is utterly incredible. If he did, a fact that neither the District Court nor the Court of Appeals found, the lesson was lost on all but the psychic *Spectrum* staffer.

The Court's second excuse for deviating from precedent is the school's interest in shielding an impressionable high school audience from material whose substance is "unsuitable for immature audiences. . . ."

Tinker teaches us that the state educator's undeniable, and undeniably vital, mandate to inculcate moral and political values is not a general warrant to act as "thought police" stifling discussion of all but state-approved topics and advocacy of all but the official position. Otherwise educators could transform students into "closed-circuit recipients of only that which the State chooses to communicate," *Tinker*, and cast a perverse and impermissible "pall of orthodoxy over the classroom," *Keyishian v. Board of Regents.* Thus, the State cannot constitutionally prohibit its high school students from recounting in the locker room "the particulars of [their] teen-age sexual activity," nor even from advocating "irresponsible se[x]" or other presumed abominations of "the shared values of a civilized social order." Even in its capacity as educator the State may not assume an Orwellian "guardianship of the public mind," *Thomas v. Collins.*

School Sponsorship Does Not Justify Thought Control

The mere fact of school sponsorship does not, as the Court suggests, license such thought control in the high school, whether through school suppression of disfavored viewpoints or through official assessment of topic sensitivity. The former would constitute unabashed and unconstitutional viewpoint discrimination, as well as an impermissible infringement of the students' "'right to receive information and ideas,'" [*Board of Education v. Pico*]. Just as a school board may not purge its state-funded library of all books that "'offen[d] [its] social, political and moral tastes,'" school officials may not, out of like motivation, discriminatorily excise objectionable ideas from a student publication. The State's prerogative to dissolve the student newspaper entirely (or to limit its subject matter) no more entitles it to dictate which viewpoints students may express on its pages, than the State's prerogative to close down the schoolhouse entitles it to prohibit the nondisruptive expression of antiwar sentiment within its gates.

Official censorship of student speech on the ground that it addresses "potentially sensitive topics" is, for related reasons, equally impermissible. I would not begrudge an educator the authority to limit the substantive scope of a school-sponsored publication to a certain, objectively definable topic, such as literary criticism, school sports, or an overview of the school year. Unlike those determinate limitations, "potential topic sensitivity" is a vaporous nonstandard. . . .

The case before us aptly illustrates how readily school officials (and courts) can camouflage viewpoint discrimination as the "mere" protection of students from sensitive topics. Among the grounds that the Court advances to uphold the principal's censorship of one of the articles was the potential sensitivity of "teenage sexual activity." Yet the District Court specifically found that the principal "did not, as a matter of principle, oppose discussion of said topi[c] in *Spectrum*." That much is also clear from the same principal's approval of the "squeal law" article on the same page, dealing forthrightly with "teenage sexuality," "the use of contraceptives by teenagers," and "teenage pregnancy." If topic sensitivity were the true basis of the principal's decision, the two articles should have been equally objectionable. It is much more likely that the objectionable article was objectionable because of the viewpoint it

73

expressed: It might have been read (as the majority apparently does) to advocate "irresponsible sex."

The School Could Disclaim Ideas Without Censorship

The sole concomitant of school sponsorship that might conceivably justify the distinction that the Court draws between sponsored and nonsponsored student expression is the risk "that the views of the individual speaker [might be] erroneously attributed to the school." Of course, the risk of erroneous attribution inheres in any student expression, including "personal expression" that, like the armbands in *Tinker*, "happens to occur on the school premises." Nevertheless, the majority is certainly correct that indicia of school sponsorship increase the likelihood of such attribution, and that state educators may therefore have a legitimate interest in dissociating themselves from student speech.

But "'[e]ven though the governmental purpose be legitimate and substantial, that purpose cannot be pursued by means that broadly stifle fundamental personal liberties when the end can be more narrowly achieved.'" *Keyishian v. Board of Regents*, (quoting *Shelton v. Tucker*). Dissociative means short of censorship are available to the school. It could, for example, require the student activity to publish a disclaimer, such as the "Statement of Policy" that *Spectrum* published each school year announcing that "[a]ll . . . editorials appearing in this newspaper reflect the opinions of the *Spectrum* staff, which are not necessarily shared by the administrators or faculty of Hazelwood East," or it could simply issue its own response clarifying the official position on the matter and explaining why the student position is wrong. Yet, without so much as acknowledging the less oppressive alternatives, the Court approves of brutal censorship.

Since the censorship served no legitimate pedagogical purpose, it cannot by any stretch of the imagination have been designed to prevent "materia[l] disrup[tion of] classwork," *Tinker*. Nor did the censorship fall within the category that *Tinker* described as necessary to prevent student expression from "inva[ding] the rights of others," ibid. If that term is to have any content, it must be limited to rights that are protected by law. "Any yardstick less exacting than [that] could result in school officials curtailing speech at the slightest fear of disturbance," a prospect that would be completely at odds with this Court's pronouncement that the "undifferentiated fear or apprehension of disturbance is not enough [even in the public school context] to overcome the right to freedom of expression." *Tinker*. And, as the Court of Appeals correctly reasoned, whatever journalistic impropriety these articles may have contained, they could not conceivably be tortious, much less criminal.

Finally, even if the majority were correct that the principal could constitutionally have censored the objectionable material, I would emphatically object to the brutal manner in which he did so. Where "[t]he separation of legitimate from illegitimate speech calls for more sensitive tools" *Speiser v. Randall*, the principal used a paper shredder. He objected to some material in two articles, but excised six entire articles. He did not so much as inquire into obvious alternatives, such as precise deletions or additions (one of which had already been made), rearranging the layout, or delaying publication. Such unthinking contempt for individual rights is intolerable from any state official. It is particularly insidious from one to whom the public entrusts the task of inculcating in its youth an appreciation for the cherished democratic liberties that our Constitution guarantees.

The Court opens its analysis in this case by purporting to reaffirm *Tinker*'s time-tested proposition that public school students "do not 'shed their constitutional rights to freedom of speech or expression at the schoolhouse gate.'" (quoting *Tinker*). That is an ironic introduction to an opinion that denudes high school students of much of the First Amendment protection that *Tinker* itself prescribed. Instead of "teach[ing] children to respect the diversity of ideas that is fundamental to the American system," *Board of Education v. Pico*, and "that our Constitution is a living reality, not parchment preserved under glass," *Shanley v. Northeast Independent School Dist.*, the Court today "teach[es] youth to discount important principles of our government as mere platitudes." *West Virginia Board of Education v. Barnette*. The young men and women of Hazelwood East expected a civics lesson, but not the one the Court teaches them today.

> *"The three students ... were the only ones who acted responsibly. They stood up for their rights, the action that gives meaning to the Constitution."*

Students Stood Up for Their Rights, Giving Meaning to the Constitution

Steve Vissner

In this viewpoint, which was written after the Supreme Court had heard the case of Hazelwood v. Kuhlmeier *but before it ruled, Steve Vissner (then a reporter for the* Jackson Sun*) tells what really happened at Hazelwood East High School. The principal said he had censored stories written for the school newspaper to protect the privacy of the people they dealt with, but, Vissner says, his real reason was that he knew the school board would think they were too controversial. The teacher who had been the adviser for the paper, Bob Stergos, was also in trouble with the school board, and quit his job shortly before the stories were due to be published because he was ordered not to let students write anything critical of its policies. The school administrators refused to show the stories to the public, but later, when they were published in a city newspaper, people were not upset by them. In Vissner's opinion, the students were the only ones who acted responsibly.*

On October 13 [1987] the Supreme Court heard one of the most important First Amendment cases to be tried under the Reagan Administration. The Court will rule whether school principals can quash a free press in public schools.

The Hazelwood School District et al. v. Kuhlmeier et al. goes to the core of a school's mission to prepare students socially and politically for democracy. Cathy Kuhlmeier, Leslie Smart and Leanne Tippett-West sued the Hazelwood, Missouri, school district in 1983 when Robert Reynolds, principal of Hazelwood East High School, censored a two-page special section on teen-age problems from *Spectrum*, their school newspaper. The relatively tame stories examined such subjects as divorce, runaways and teen-age pregnancy. The young women suspected Reynolds wanted to cover up problems that might tarnish the school's excellent reputation. They were only partly right.

Hazelwood is the latest volley in a battle waged since the 1960s: students' rights versus principals' authority. The Supreme Court ruled in 1969 in *Tinker v. The Des Moines Independent Community School District* that principals may not stifle speech unless it is libelous, legally obscene or would disrupt the educational process. Lower courts soon applied the ruling to school newspapers, arguing that those constitute public forums for expression protected by the First Amendment.

Principal Said He Censored the Stories to Protect Privacy

Hazelwood authorities, however, learned from their colleagues' failures. Although they also claimed a right to control the paper, they offered the most benign reasons for their actions. Reynolds testified that he had "edited" in order to protect innocent students and families whose identities hadn't been effectively concealed. The divorce story, for example, initially quoted by name a student describing the causes of her parents' divorce. Student editors later deleted the name, but Reynolds, who saw only an uncorrected galley proof, testified that the story was an invasion of privacy.

Federal Judge John Nangle, who first heard the case, ruled that *Spectrum* wasn't a public forum and that Reynolds's actions were reasonable, since he had not sought to stifle controversy. Nangle concluded that Hazelwood officials could censor articles in a school newspaper to avoid the impression that school authorities endorsed the sexual values presented. The Eighth District Court of Appeals overturned his ruling.

In fact Reynolds censored the stories for the oldest of bureaucratic reasons: to cover his ass. "I knew darn well those articles weren't going to fly—I didn't have to look at them twice," Reynolds told me in 1985 after the trial "The board and administration, even though they're good law-abiding citizens, want things run in their district the way they want them run. They hire people who can do that, and when they can't do it any longer, they get rid of them."

Bob Stergos, a journalism teacher, advised *Spectrum* from September 1981 to April 1983. He approved the articles on teen-age problems but left the school before they were due to be published. Howard Emerson, a journalism teacher from Hazelwood Central High School, oversaw the last two issues of *Spectrum*. He viewed Stergos as a brilliant teacher victimized by the district. He had seen it happen before. Emerson was smarter than most; he quit advising school newspapers and stuck with the yearbook.

How Controversial Were the Stories?

When Emerson saw the stories, he chose not to fight. The stories were too controversial for the conservative administrators—even though they elicited only yawns when the now-defunct *St. Louis Globe-Democrat* published them two years later in response to community curiosity. When the principal saw the galley proofs, Emerson said, he ordered the entire paper killed. Emerson then suggested killing only the two pages containing the stories, and Reynolds agreed.

The story that most incensed the principal concerned three anonymous Hazelwood East students who had got pregnant. The girls presented an optimistic view of their future, which Reynolds labeled an advocacy position. He apparently didn't think an article that outlined the dismal consequences facing sexually active teen-agers who shunned birth control, another that discussed the high failure rate of teen-age marriages or a third that attempted to warn of the scars divorce can leave on kids would dampen any enthusiasm for teen-age pregnancy among readers. The stories quoted students, teachers, counselors, local authorities and magazines and were designed both to warn students and tell them where they could get help.

School administrators refused to discuss the specifics of the stories with the public or faculty. Some teachers and Parent-Teacher Association members said the administration avoided debate by suggesting that the stories were suitable for the *National Enquirer*. "They kept saying, 'If you could only see the stories'—which of course they would never show us—'you would know how bad they were,'" one PTA member said. "Well, that made us really curious, but when we finally saw them printed in the *Globe*, we thought, What was all the fuss about? I don't think anyone was upset over them."

It had been a difficult year for Reynolds. His boss, associate superintendent Francis Huss, has a penchant for abusing journalism advisers and dressing down principals who can't control them. "Huss wants to approve everything, absolutely everything, and he's just a very domineering personality," said one longtime teacher at Hazelwood East.

"Teachers know . . . that he does have the power if he wants to use it," said another Hazelwood East teacher, "and this person will get hired and this person will get fired, so don't let him catch you laughing in his face."

Journalism Teacher Had to Quit His Job

Huss, who oversaw the district's high schools, was critical of Reynolds because the principal was having trouble with Stergos, who believed that teaching journalism required that students examine school issues and expose problems. Stergos, at 26, was politically naive and a tad self-righteous: a true believer who thought his excellence put him above office politics or even misguided authority.

The semester before, students had written a series of articles on grading inconsistencies and fairness regarding ratings of class participation, as well as comparisons of coaches' salaries (coaches of women's sports were paid less). They weren't stories Huss liked, so he came over to browbeat the journalism adviser.

"I walked in and the first thing he said to me was, 'Do you want to keep your job?'" Stergos told me, a statement Reynolds later corroborated. "He said, 'I don't care how you do it, but you will not allow those students to question board policy again.' What he was subtly trying to tell me was that there are ways you can steer students away from controversial issues. But if I did that, I wouldn't be doing my job."

Stergos in effect told Huss to go to hell, which hardly pleased the administrator. Reynolds says he broke the deadlock by ordering Stergos to forgo any controversial articles and submit to prior review: "So I finally told Bob, in January, whenever it was, 'I'm going to see the paper first. I've never done that before, and I don't know that I believe in it, but for your sake and my fanny, I'm going to do that.'"

In court, while Reynolds defended privacy and fairness, Huss claimed Stergos had been reprimanded only for violating the curriculum. But the district curriculum guide for journalism states that "students will be able to . . . research a subject in-depth to write a documented analysis of a school problem or issue." Reynolds later admitted to me that the administration possibly had been closer to violating the curriculum than had the adviser.

During the January meeting with Reynolds, Stergos kept mum about the planned articles on teen-age pregnancy and stomped back to his classroom. The adviser correctly discerned that his free-press and probably his teaching days were over. (Reynolds told me he planned to offer Stergos the choice of his teaching career: no controversy or no contract. "I was going to make him an offer he couldn't refuse," the principal joked.) Stergos soon began interviewing for other jobs and found one as a consultant. The district released him from his contract and he left Hazelwood East two weeks before the articles were to appear. "I just felt there was no use fighting city hall," he said.

Stergos wasn't the first Hazelwood East journalism adviser to fall by the wayside, and he wouldn't be the last; both his predecessor's and successor's tours ended bitterly. "Some of the bitterest people I've ever met have been advisers of school newspapers," said a Hazelwood East teacher who knew all three advisers. "They are some of the most conscientious, hard-working, well-intentioned people as far as I can observe, but they are caught in so many tensions. All the school wanted was good show, good image and for them not to make any waves."

The American Civil Liberties Union Took the Case

After Reynolds censored the articles, the students called Stergos. He advised them to go to the American Civil Liberties Union, which took their case. Stergos soon found out that he wasn't beyond the reach of Hazelwood East administrators. Reynolds threatened to get Stergos's teaching certificate revoked unless he "stopped coaching the kids." The school board declined to pursue the action. Reynolds told me he went after

the teaching certificate because he suspected Stergos was using the students as pawns to settle his grudge with the school. Maybe he was right. In any event, Stergos believed scholastic journalism meant more than profiles of prom queens. He taught the values of a free press.

To city reporters and to me, the administrators spouted platitudes about responsible journalism and irresponsible students. The kids, they implied, weren't mature enough for First Amendment freedom; school authorities should judge what information was fit to print. But the three students, Kuhlmeier, Smart and Tippett-West, were the only ones who acted responsibly. They stood up for their rights, the action that gives meaning to the Constitution. During this year of Constitutional celebration [the 200th anniversary of the Constitution] it will be interesting to see if those rights are reaffirmed.

"No written constitution can save [the First Amendment] if most of the present generation of students turn out to be indifferent to free speech when they become adults."

Young People Must Not Become Indifferent to Free Speech Issues

Nat Hentoff

Nat Hentoff is a columnist for the Washington Post *and the* Village Voice. *He is the author of several books and is a well-known advocate of free speech. In the following viewpoint he expresses his dismay at the Supreme Court's decision in* Hazelwood v. Kuhlmeier, *which gave schools the right to censor official student publications and anything else done under school sponsorship. He says that although the Court was concerned that people might mistakenly think the views of the students were endorsed by the school, this could be avoided without censorship by publishing disclaimers. However, Hentoff points out, a free, independent student press is still possible because it is legal for students to publish their own underground newspapers and distribute them at school. In his opinion, if Americans now in school become indifferent to the issue, the constitutional protection of free speech cannot be kept alive.*

Nat Hentoff, "School Newspapers and the Supreme Court," *School Library Journal*, vol. 34, March 1988, pp. 114–16. Copyright © 1988. Reproduced from School Library Journal. A Cahners/R. R. Bowker Publication, by permission.

Since *The First Freedom* was originally published [in 1980], there has been one radical change of interpretation by the Supreme Court with regard to the First Amendment. The target was American public school students and their rights of free expression.

In 1986, there were signs of what was to come. In *Bethel School District v. Matthew Fraser*, the High Court ruled that student free-speech rights do not include the right to engage in "indecent speech." Matthew Fraser, a senior with high grades who had never gotten into trouble, had made a nominating speech on behalf of a friend running for class office at his high school. "I know a man who is firm—he's firm in his pants, he's firm in his shirt, his character is firm—but most of all, his belief in you, the students of Bethel, is firm," Fraser had said.

A majority of the Court described his talk as containing "explicit sexual metaphors." It was therefore "indecent" and was not—so far as students were concerned—protected by the First Amendment. But "indecent speech" is a very vague term, and the license it gives principals to censor students can be very easily abused.

At the beginning of 1988, a majority of the Court went even further to cut down on student free-speech rights that had previously been guaranteed by the 1969 Magna Carta of student rights: *Tinker v. Des Moines Independent School District*.

The case, *Hazelwood School District v. Kuhlmeier*, began when the principal of a high school in a St. Louis suburb removed two pages from a forthcoming issue of the student paper, without telling the editors and reporters. Six articles were censored thereby, but the two he was really after had to do with teenage pregnancy and the effects of divorce on children.

Both stories included interviews with students at Hazelwood, but no names were used. Nonetheless, the principal said that some of the students might have been identifiable—

though they willingly gave the interviews—and that a father in the article on divorce should have had a chance to reply. But the father was also not named. In addition, the principal considered the articles "inappropriate, personal, sensitive, and unsuitable for student readers."

In his very broad opinion for the Court's majority, Justice Byron White ruled that principals can now censor just about any student speech, written or oral, that is not officially approved. Students still retain some free speech in places like the lunchroom, or in classes where teachers believe that a goal of education is independent thinking.

Schools Can Censor Anything They Sponsor

There is no ambiguity about this drastic removal of First Amendment rights for public school students. Justice White states that educators have censoring authority "over school-sponsored publications, theatrical productions, and other expressive activities that students, parents, and members of the public might reasonably perceive to bear the imprimatur of the school."

Whatever appears to be sponsored by the school can be censored.

But what are the criteria by which principals will decide what to ban? They can suppress anything that is inconsistent with the school's "basic educational mission." There is no further definition of that term, and so there can be as many definitions of that vague and woolly phrase as there are principals and boards of education. Moreover, each definition can change by the day. In the "real world," for which students presumably are being educated, there can be no punishment unless it is clear, in advance, what the crime is.

Justice White went on to rule that student speech can also be censored if it "associates the school with any position other than neutrality on matters of political controversy." Students, including those old enough to vote—and there are many in

the schools—are now in peril if they write opinion articles on political issues or candidates. Yet, speech about how we govern ourselves is at the core of First Amendment values. The Soviet Union's cultural attachés in the United States must be much bemused by this decision.

In dissent, Justice William Brennan Jr., also speaking for Justices Thurgood Marshall and Harry Blackmun, accused the majority of his colleagues of approving "brutal censorship" and giving educators the power to act as "thought police." Justice Brennan denounced, too, the principal of Hazelwood High School for his "unthinking contempt for individual rights," and sharply criticized the majority decision of the Court for denuding "high school students for much of the First Amendment protection that the Tinker case prescribed.

"Instead of teaching children to respect the diversity of ideas that is fundamental to the American system, the Court today teaches youth to discount important principles of our government as mere platitudes." And, he noted, the Court majority failed to teach American students "that our Constitution is a living reality, not parchment preserved under glass."

The day after the *Hazelwood* decision came down, a high school senior in Dayton, Ohio, who is the editor of the school paper, said to me: "I go into my government class, and I'm told that, as an American, I'm guaranteed certain basic rights. Now I go into my journalism class and I'm told that the most important of those rights has been taken away from me."

Schools Could Print Disclaimers

The majority of the Court had been concerned that no one should mistakenly regard student speech as carrying the school's imprimatur—the school's sponsorship—when the school wants to disassociate itself from what was said or printed. There are a number of ways, however, to accomplish that end without squashing the First Amendment rights of the students.

For instance, a disclaimer can be printed in the student paper. *The Scroll*, the newspaper at R. Nelson Snider High School in Fort Wayne, Indiana, states in every issue: "Editorials in *The Scroll* do *not* represent the opinions of the administration . . . Vigorous and free practice of First Amendment rights are guaranteed to *The Scroll* and its staff. *The Scroll* is free of any censorship."

In Dade County (Miami) Florida, the school board, since 1981, has stated, as official policy, that the student newspapers are not censored. The students operate under a set of guidelines agreed on by faculty, administrators, students, and a professional journalist. While the faculty adviser acts as a guide, all the final decisions are made by the student editors. The school newspapers in Dade County run solid investigative pieces on drugs, "safe sex," and politics. Despite the Supreme Court's decision in *Hazelwood*, the school officials in Miami do not intend to turn the school papers back to the principals. The students have proved that if they are expected to be responsible, they will be.

Elsewhere in the country, however, many principals were delighted, even exhilarated, at gaining full control of what's said or written by their students. In one California high school paper, an article on AIDS was censored within an hour after the Supreme Court decision was announced on the radio. And, a Missouri school administrator said that the High Court had made his day.

Underground Papers Are Legal

But there is hope for those student journalists who know that the only way to understand the First Amendment is to use it. As the legendary labor organizer, Joe Hill, used to say: "Don't mourn. Organize."

Nothing in the *Hazelwood* decision prevents public school students from starting their own underground or alternative paper. By previous Supreme Court rulings, students can distribute unofficial newspapers in school—subject to time, place, and manner restrictions. That is, you can't give out the papers in the middle of a geography class, but you can distribute them before school or maybe during lunch hour. So a free, independent student press is still possible.

It is possible, however, that *Hazelwood* will eventually be reversed. The Supreme Court does change its mind, as it did in the case of the children of Jehovah's Witnesses who refused to salute the flag. New members may understand far better than today's majority how vital it is that education really be a preparation for living in a free society. So we may get a future majority who will agree with today's dissenting Justice William Brennan Jr. that "the educator's undeniable . . . mandate to inculcate moral and political values is not a general warrant to act as 'thought police' stifling discussion of all but state-approved topics, and advocacy of all but the official position."

As for the future of the First Amendment for all Americans, a warning by Judge Learned Hand remains true: "Liberty lies in the hearts and minds of men and women. When it dies there, no constitution, no law, no court can save it."

Students Must Not Be Indifferent

If those Americans who are now in school do not come to see the First Amendment as a *personal* liberty, worth fighting for, then no written constitution can save it if most of the present generation of students turn out to be indifferent to free speech when they become adults.

And for students, the fight for free speech can go on, even under the chill of the *Hazelwood* decision, for there *are* principals who can be brought to an understanding of what an *American* education ought to be if the Constitution is to be kept alive.

Throughout our history, as we have seen, the First Amendment has survived—often against great dangers—because there has always been a nucleus of Americans who recognize that without these quintessential freedoms of religion, speech, and press, the United States would soon be like many other countries in the world—a nation where the people are told what to think and what to say by their rulers. This is what the present majority of the Supreme Court would like to have happen in our high schools.

In 1838, Abraham Lincoln asked, "At what point shall we expect the approach of danger? By what means shall we fortify against it? Shall we expect some transatlantic military giant to step the ocean and crush us at a blow? Never! All the armies of Europe. Asia and Africa combined . . . could not, by force, take a drink from the Ohio [river], or make a track on the Blue Ridge [mountain], in . . . a thousand years . . . If destruction be our lot, we must ourselves be its author and finisher. As a nation of freemen [and freewomen], we must live for all times, or die by suicide."

The only people who can destroy our liberties—the First Amendment being foremost among them, for how is it possible to protect the others without free speech—are ourselves—by not using and defending those liberties.

It is also vital always to keep in mind that the Constitution is indeed a *living* document. During the 1987 Bicentennial Year, Thurgood Marshall reminded Americans that the framers of the Constitution hardly created a perfect document. As far as blacks and women were concerned, it was appallingly flawed. Blacks were still enslaved, and neither were "persons" under the Constitution. It required, Thurgood Marshall emphasized, "several [constitutional] amendments, a civil war, and momentous social transformations to attain the system of constitutional government—and its respect for the individual freedoms and human rights—we hold as fundamental today. And so we must be careful, when focusing on the events which took place in Philadelphia two centuries ago, that we not overlook the momentous events which followed."

There may yet be momentous events to come.

"As a result of the Hazelwood *decision, secondary schools have censored student speech far more rampantly in the past decade than in previous years."*

The Court's Decision Has Resulted in Curtailment of Students' First Amendment Rights

Mark J. Fiore

At the time the following viewpoint was written, Mark J. Fiore was a law student at the University of Pennsylvania. In it, he describes how the right of students to free speech established by the Supreme Court in Tinker v. Des Moines *was modified by the later cases* Bethel v. Fraser *and* Hazelwood v. Kuhlmeier. *Since* Hazelwood, *Fiore reports, federal courts and most state courts have applied the precedent it set, and have rarely ruled against schools in free speech cases. This has been true not only where verbal speech is involved, but also in cases involving student attire and school mascots. A few states have passed laws giving students broader rights than they would have under* Hazelwood. *But on the whole, high schools have censored student speech much more than in the past, partly because students are now writing more hard-hitting stories.*

Mark J. Fiore, "Trampling the 'Marketplace of Ideas': The Case Against Extending *Hazelwood* to College Campuses," *University of Pennsylvania Law Review*, vol. 150, 2002, pp. 1918–30. Copyright © 2002 University of Pennsylvania Law School. Reproduced by permission.

The First Amendment free speech rights of students in secondary schools have been shaped largely by three Supreme Court cases: *Tinker v. Des Moines Independent School District, Bethel School District v. Fraser,* and *Hazelwood.* While *Tinker* started from the premise that "[i]t can hardly be argued that either students or teachers shed their constitutional rights to freedom of speech or expression at the schoolhouse gate," the Court has limited those rights sharply in *Fraser* and *Hazelwood.*

Tinker is the proper starting point for an examination of the First Amendment rights of public school students. The dispute in *Tinker* arose when three students in Des Moines, Iowa, wore black armbands to school to protest the Vietnam War. When the schools' principals got wind of the plan, they adopted a policy that any student wearing an armband would be asked to remove it or face suspension. Aware of the policy, the students wore their armbands to school, resulting in suspensions until they agreed to return without their armbands. Claiming a violation of their First Amendment rights, the students sued.

In a 7-2 decision, the Supreme Court found a First Amendment violation. The Court recognized that First Amendment rights must be balanced. "in light of the special characteristics of the school environment," with the rights of school officials "to prescribe and control conduct in the schools." Weighing these conflicting propositions, the Court held that student speech may only be regulated if it "would substantially interfere with the work of the school or impinge upon the rights of other students."

Applying this standard, the Court found no evidence of disruption. The Court noted, for example, that "[o]nly a few of the 18,000 students in the school system wore the black armbands," and "[o]nly five students were suspended." Highlighting the constitutional importance of free speech, the Court stated:

In our system, students may not be regarded as closed circuit recipients of only that which the State chooses to communicate. They may not be confined to the expression of
those sentiments that are officially approved. In the absence
of a specific showing of constitutionally valid reasons to
regulate their speech, students are entitled to freedom of expression of their views.

Bethel School District v. Fraser

The broad free speech rights granted to public school students
under *Tinker* began facing restrictions with the Supreme
Court's *Fraser* decision nearly two decades later. In *Fraser*, the
Court considered the free speech rights of a public high school
student who had delivered a sexually suggestive speech during
a school assembly. After the student, Matthew N. Fraser, delivered his speech, he faced suspension for violating a school
policy prohibiting the use of obscene language. Fraser served a
two-day suspension and filed suit.

The Supreme Court upheld Fraser's punishment by a 7-2
decision, and distinguished *Tinker* by noting that the expression in *Tinker* could not be construed associated with the
school, while Fraser's speech was given as part of an official
school activity. The Court further distinguished the speech in
Tinker as "political" speech, thus reasoning that the *Tinker*
standard need not apply to nonpolitical speech such as
Fraser's. Rather, the Court emphasized that "schools must
teach by example the shared values of a civilized social order"
and, as a result, can prohibit "lewd, indecent, or offensive
speech."

The Court used similar reasoning two years later in *Hazelwood*. While not explicitly overruling *Tinker*, the Court, in a
5-3 decision, developed a far more stringent First Amendment
standard for certain public school speech. Of concern to the
Court was the decision by the principal of Hazelwood East
High School to censor two pages of an issue of the school's
student newspaper, *Spectrum*. The newspaper, produced as

part of a journalism course, was subsidized largely with funds from the school district and was subject to various oversight mechanisms. When the newspaper staff submitted proofs of the issue to the principal, he ordered the removal of two articles, one describing three Hazelwood East students' experiences with pregnancy, and the other discussing the impact of divorce on students at the school.

School Newspapers Are Not Public Forums

Adopting a public forum analysis, the Supreme Court held that the principal's actions did not violate the students' First Amendment rights. While the Court acknowledged the broad First Amendment school rights granted in *Tinker*, it also recognized both the restrictions placed on those rights in *Fraser* and the need for schools to instill civic values in students. In reaching its conclusion, the Court determined that the school newspaper could not be considered a public forum. In previous cases, the Court found three types of forums, each of which has its own First Amendment standards. In a traditional public forum, such as a public park, the government has a very limited ability to limit free speech rights. Only those restrictions that are narrowly drawn to serve a compelling state interest will pass First Amendment scrutiny. On the opposite end are nonpublic forums, such as military bases and prisons, in which the government may impose extensive restrictions on First Amendment rights, so long as the restrictions are reasonable. Finally, in the middle are limited public forums, where the government's rights are as limited as those in a public forum once it is determined that the government has opened up the forum for expressive use.

Applying this analysis, the Court in *Hazelwood* stated that "school facilities may be deemed to be public forums only if school authorities have 'by policy or by practice' opened those facilities 'for indiscriminate use by the general public.'" The Court explained that "'[t]he government does not create a public forum by inaction or by permitting limited discourse, but only by intentionally opening a nontraditional forum for public discourse.'" With this public forum standard established, the Court turned to the intent of Hazelwood East officials. First, the Court noted that *Spectrum's* purpose was largely educational, in part because it was produced by a journalism class taught by a faculty member during regular class hours and for academic credit. The Court also emphasized that the course's teacher had significant involvement in the newspaper's production, ranging from the selection of editors to the editing of stories. The Court found additional evidence insufficient to show that the school intended *Spectrum* to be a public forum. For example, a policy statement published in an issue of *Spectrum*, declaring that "*Spectrum*, as a student-press publication, accepts all rights implied by the First Amendment," did not reflect an intent of the school's administration to expand students' free speech rights by converting the newspaper into a public forum.

Personal vs. School-Sponsored Speech

The Court then proceeded to distinguish *Tinker* on the grounds that the speech in *Tinker* was personal while the speech in *Hazelwood* was "school-sponsored." Addressing the distinction, the Court stated:

> Educators are entitled to exercise greater control over this second form of student expression [school-sponsored speech] to assure that participants learn whatever lessons the activity is designed to teach, that readers or listeners are not exposed to material that may be inappropriate for their level of maturity, and that the views of the individual speaker are not erroneously attributed to the school. Hence, a school may in its capacity as publisher of a school newspaper or producer of a school play "disassociate itself," [*Bethel Sch. Dist. v.*] *Fraser*, [(1986)], not only from speech that would "substantially interfere with [its] work . . . or impinge upon the fights of other students," *Tinker* [*v. Des Moines Indep.*

Sch. Dist.], [(1969)], but also from speech that is, for example, ungrammatical, poorly written, inadequately researched, biased or prejudiced, vulgar or profane, or unsuitable for immature audiences.

The Court also emphasized that schools must consider the maturity of the audience exposed to the student speech and must perform their role as one of the principal instruments in instilling cultural values in children. With such principles in mind, the Court announced a new standard for evaluating the constitutionality of "school-sponsored" speech, such as that found in *Hazelwood*, holding that "educators do not offend the First Amendment by exercising editorial control over the style and content of student speech in school-sponsored expressive activities so long as their actions are reasonably related to legitimate pedagogical concerns."

With this new standard in hand, the Court found that Hazelwood East's principal acted reasonably in censoring *Spectrum*. Addressing the potential identification of the girls in the pregnancy article, the Court stated that the principal "could reasonably have feared that the article violated whatever pledge of anonymity had been given to the pregnant students." In addition, the principal reasonably could have believed that the "frank talk" on sexual topics in the pregnancy article "was inappropriate in a school-sponsored publication distributed to 14-year-old freshmen and presumably taken home to be read by students' even younger brothers and sisters."

Public School Students' Free Speech Rights in the Lower Federal Courts

The lower federal courts and most state courts have applied the *Hazelwood* standard faithfully. Consequently, student speech is now significantly circumscribed in the federal courts. Indeed, the courts rarely find against schools in student free speech cases, notwithstanding the variety of contexts in which they are brought. The Third Circuit, for example, indicated in

Brody v. Spang that a public high school graduation ceremony is unlikely to be considered a public forum. The court followed *Hazelwood* because the "process for setting the format and contents of a graduation ceremony are more likely to resemble the tightly controlled school newspaper policies at issue in *Hazelwood* than the broad group access policies considered in [other relevant Supreme Court cases]."

Even when the expression at issue involves no vocal speech, such as the attire students wear in school, First Amendment rights in schools have been curtailed. The Sixth Circuit, for example, upheld a high school administrator's decision prohibiting a student from wearing Marilyn Manson T-shirts. Applying the tripartite structure of *Tinker, Fraser*, and *Hazelwood*, the court found that the shirts were offensive and could cause a substantial disruption in the school and thus held that the school constitutionally could prohibit them. The Seventh Circuit reached a similar conclusion in *Baxter v. Vigo County School Corp.* when it upheld the decision of a school principal who prohibited a student from wearing shirts with messages such as "Unfair Grades" and "Racism." The Ninth Circuit, by contrast, granted broader First Amendment freedom to students when it upheld their rights to wear buttons in support of striking teachers.

Hazelwood also has come up in the context of school mascots. In *Crosby v. Holsinger*, the Fourth Circuit upheld a high school principal's decision to eliminate "Johnny Reb" as the school's mascot because it offended black students and parents. The court held that, under *Hazelwood* a school need not associate itself with certain expression. The court stated:

> A school mascot or symbol bears the stamp of approval of the school itself. Therefore, school authorities are free to disassociate the school from such a symbol because of educational concerns. Here, Principal Holsinger received complaints that Johnny Reb offended blacks and limited their

participation in school activities, so he eliminated the symbol based on legitimate concerns.

As the Fourth Circuit's holding thus makes clear, the lower federal courts freely apply *Hazelwood* to many forms of speech.

Public School Students' Free Speech Rights in the State Courts

In the state courts, meanwhile, public school students free speech rights have been limited in some jurisdictions to the same extent as in the federal courts, while they are broader in other state jurisdictions. Two states, Arkansas and Kansas, have codified laws that grant public school student publications broader First Amendment rights than they would be entitled to under *Hazelwood*. Four additional states have passed laws that not only give broader fights to student publications, but to all other forms of student expression as well. Of those states, only California had codified the *Tinker* standard prior to *Hazelwood*. Colorado, Iowa, and Massachusetts provide similar free speech rights for public school students. Two additional states, Pennsylvania and Washington, have free speech regulations in their administrative codes. Since *Hazelwood* became law, however, dozens of states have considered legislation that would reject its holding. Only a few states have passed such legislation into law.

Censorship in Secondary Schools

As a result of the *Hazelwood* decision, secondary schools have censored student speech far more rampantly in the past decade than in previous years. According to the Student Press Law Center, a non-profit organization that provides legal support to public school and college media, the number of inquiries it receives each year has soared since the mid 1980s. In 1986, the Center reported hearing of 548 cases of censorship. That Statistic nearly tripled to 1588 in 1997. In 1999, the number of inquiries to the Center reached 1624. Of those inquiries, 367 came from high school journalists or their advisors, an increase of fourteen percent from 1998. Mike Hiestand, an attorney for the Center, attributed the rise in part to the increasing tenacity of student journalists. "Students are now writing more hard-hitting stories, and administrations seem to be cracking down on them," Hiestand said. "They're not just writing about football games and proms anymore."

One such instance arose in State College, Pennsylvania, in 1998, when a high school newspaper sought to publish a controversial story about students allegedly drinking at the school's homecoming dance. The award-winning newspaper, the *Lions' Digest*, had a history of publishing probing journalism on such topics as birth control, drugs, and homosexuality. Given that history, the staff was especially taken aback when the school administration ordered the newspaper not to publish its homecoming story. The administration claimed protection of students' privacy; the newspaper cried censorship. Whatever the reason, the story was killed. "I guess I've learned that, when you look back at all of this, you can't cross the administration," said Mike Conti, Jr., then the newspaper's editor-in-chief. "They will always have the final say." Most federal courts appear to agree.

CHAPTER 3

Affirming That Internet Pornography Cannot Be Banned Outright

Case Overview

Ashcroft v. Free Speech Coalition (2002)

In 1996 Congress, concerned by the proliferation of child pornography on the Internet, passed the Child Pornography Prevention Act (CPPA). This law extended the definition of child pornography to cover not only sexually explicit photos of real children, but "any visual depiction, including any photograph, film, video, picture, or computer or computer-generated image or picture" that "is, or appears to be, of a minor engaging in sexually explicit conduct." The Free Speech Coalition, an adult-entertainment trade association, challenged this law in court, saying that its wording was too vague and would prohibit works that are protected under the First Amendment. The District Court disagreed, but on appeal the Circuit Court ruled that the wording did indeed cover materials that were neither obscene nor produced through exploitation of children—the only two exceptions to the First Amendment that apply to pornography. Attorney General John Ashcroft, representing the government, requested review by the Supreme Court.

The Court decided that although the CPPA was designed to prohibit virtual child pornography—images produced on a computer without using real children, or porn movies made with young-looking actors—it would also extend to Hollywood movies, including some Academy Award winners and even *Romeo and Juliet*. The characters in many movies are under eighteen, even though the actors who play them are older than they look. And, the Court pointed out, in some states eighteen is higher than the legal age for marriage, or for consent to sexual relations. Movies about sex between teenagers often have artistic or social value. Producers would stop making such movies if they were classed with pornographers and subject to the severe penalties called for by the CPPA—which could be imposed for a single scene involving simulated sex between minors. In fact, the CPPA prohibited mere possession of such a movie.

Furthermore, the Court was not convinced by the arguments the government offered in defense of the CPPA. The law against pornography involving real children is justified because of the harm done to the children used in its production. Virtual pornography, on the other hand, does not harm any children, and the claim that it might lead to crimes against them by encouraging pedophiles is not a sufficient reason to restrict free speech. "The Court's First Amendment cases draw vital distinctions between words and deeds, between ideas and conduct," it stated. "The government may not prohibit speech because it increases the chance an unlawful act will be committed 'at some indefinite future time.'" Therefore, the CPPA was held to be unconstitutional.

Several of the justices dissented from this opinion, at least in part, arguing that there should be a law against virtual child pornography, as long as it does not also prohibit movies that are not pornographic. Chief Justice William Rehnquist dissented from the entire judgment; he believed that the wording of the CPPA was being misinterpreted. Its definition of "sexually explicit conduct," he said, really applied only to hard-core pornography because "simulated sexual intercourse" has always been part of the law against real child pornography and nobody has thought that it covers merely suggestive scenes, such as those in *Romeo and Juliet*, which Congress presumably did not intend to ban. Moreover, the CPPA was on the books at the time the award-winning movies named by the Court were made, and their producers were not affected by it. In Chief Justice Rehnquist's opinion, the law barred only computer images that were virtually indistinguishable from images of real children, so it should have been allowed to stand.

> "The CPPA prohibits speech that records
> no crime and creates no victims by its
> production.... The harm ... depends
> upon some unquantified potential for
> subsequent criminal acts."

Majority Opinion: Prohibition of Virtual Child Pornography Would Abridge Freedom of Speech

Anthony Kennedy

Anthony Kennedy has been a justice of the U.S. Supreme Court since 1988. A strong supporter of individual liberty, he is noted for being a swing voter when differences between the conservative and liberal factions of the court result in a close decision. The following viewpoint is the opinion he delivered in the case of Ashcroft v. Free Speech Coalition, *in which the government sought to uphold a law that banned virtual child pornography— that is, pornography produced without using real children, either by computer or with young-looking adult actors. In it he explains that the law, the Child Pornography Prevention Act (CPPA), applied to much more than pornography—it banned all images that appear to depict sexual conduct involving persons under 18, including movies such as* Romeo and Juliet. *Furthermore, the existing law against child pornography is aimed at the crime of producing it and the harm to the children pictured. The government's aim with CPPA was merely to prevent crime that might occur in the future if virtual images encouraged pedo-*

Anthony Kennedy, majority decision, *John D. Ashcroft, Attorney General, et al., Petitioners v. The Free Speech Coalition et al.*, U.S. Supreme Court, April 16, 2002.

philes. The Court ruled that this aim is not sufficient to justify limiting freedom of speech, and that the law was in any case too broad because it covered movies and paintings with artistic merit.

We consider in this case whether the Child Pornography Prevention Act of 1996 (CPPA), abridges the freedom of speech. The CPPA extends the federal prohibition against child pornography to sexually explicit images that appear to depict minors but were produced without using any real children. The statute prohibits, in specific circumstances, possessing or distributing these images, which may be created by using adults who look like minors or by using computer imaging. The new technology, according to Congress, makes it possible to create realistic images of children who do not exist.

By prohibiting child pornography that does not depict an actual child, the statute goes beyond *New York v. Ferber*, which distinguished child pornography from other sexually explicit speech because of the State's interest in protecting the children exploited by the production process. As a general rule, pornography can be banned only if obscene, but under *Ferber*, pornography showing minors can be proscribed whether or not the images are obscene under the definition set forth in *Miller v. California*. *Ferber* recognized that "[t]he *Miller* standard, like all general definitions of what may be banned as obscene, does not reflect the State's particular and more compelling interest in prosecuting those who promote the sexual exploitation of children.". . .

The principal question to be resolved, then, is whether the CPPA is constitutional where it proscribes a significant universe of speech that is neither obscene under *Miller* nor child pornography under *Ferber*.

CPPA Covers Images That Do Not Involve Real Children

Before 1996, Congress defined child pornography as the type of depictions at issue in *Ferber*, images made using actual minors. The CPPA retains that prohibition and adds three other prohibited categories of speech, of which the first, Section 2256(8)(B), and the third, Section 2256(8)(D), are at issue in this case. Section 2256(8)(B) prohibits "any visual depiction, including any photograph, film, video, picture, or computer or computer-generated image or picture" that "is, or appears to be, of a minor engaging in sexually explicit conduct." The prohibition on "any visual depiction" does not depend at all on how the image is produced. The section captures a range of depictions, sometimes called "virtual child pornography," which include computer-generated images, as well as images produced by more traditional means. For instance, the literal terms of the statute embrace a Renaissance painting depicting a scene from classical mythology, a "picture" that "appears to be, of a minor engaging in sexually explicit conduct." The statute also prohibits Hollywood movies, filmed without any child actors, if a jury believes an actor "appears to be" a minor engaging in "actual or simulated . . . sexual intercourse."

These images do not involve, let alone harm, any children in the production process; but Congress decided the materials threaten children in other, less direct, ways. Pedophiles might use the materials to encourage children to participate in sexual activity. "[A] child who is reluctant to engage in sexual activity with an adult, or to pose for sexually explicit photographs, can sometimes be convinced by viewing depictions of other children 'having fun' participating in such activity." Furthermore, pedophiles might "whet their own sexual appetites" with the pornographic images, "thereby increasing the creation and distribution of child pornography and the sexual abuse and exploitation of actual children." Under these rationales, harm flows from the content of the images, not from the means of their production. In addition, Congress identified another problem created by computer-generated images: Their existence can make it harder to prosecute pornographers who do use real minors. As imaging technology improves, Congress found, it becomes more difficult to prove that a particular picture was produced using actual children. To ensure that defendants possessing child pornography using real minors cannot evade prosecution, Congress extended the ban to virtual child pornography. . . .

A law imposing criminal penalties on protected speech is a stark example of speech suppression. The CPPA's penalties are indeed severe. A first offender may be imprisoned for 15 years. A repeat offender faces a prison sentence of not less than 5 years and not more than 30 years in prison. While even minor punishments can chill protected speech, this case provides a textbook example of why we permit facial challenges [claims that a law is unconstitutional and therefore void] to statutes that burden expression. With these severe penalties in force, few legitimate movie producers or book publishers, or few other speakers in any capacity, would risk distributing images in or near the uncertain reach of this law. The Constitution gives significant protection from overbroad laws that chill speech within the First Amendment's vast and privileged sphere. Under this principle, the CPPA is unconstitutional on its face if it prohibits a substantial amount of protected expression. . . .

Congress may pass valid laws to protect children from abuse, and it has. The prospect of crime, however, by itself does not justify laws suppressing protected speech. It is also well established that speech may not be prohibited because it concerns subjects offending our sensibilities. . . .

As a general principle, the First Amendment bars the government from dictating what we see or read or speak or hear. The freedom of speech has its limits; it does not embrace certain categories of speech, including defamation, incitement, obscenity, and pornography produced with real children. While these categories may be prohibited without violating the First Amendment, none of them includes the speech prohibited by the CPPA. In his dissent from the opinion of the Court of Appeals, Judge Ferguson recognized this to be the law and proposed that virtual child pornography should be regarded as an additional category of unprotected speech. It would be necessary for us to take this step to uphold the statute.

CPPA Extends to Material That Is Not Offensive

As we have noted, the CPPA is much more than a supplement to the existing federal prohibition on obscenity. Under *Miller v. California*, the Government must prove that the work, taken as a whole, appeals to the prurient interest, is patently offensive in light of community standards, and lacks serious literary, artistic, political, or scientific value. The CPPA, however, extends to images that appear to depict a minor engaging in sexually explicit activity without regard to the *Miller* requirements. The materials need not appeal to the prurient interest. Any depiction of sexually explicit activity, no matter how it is presented, is proscribed. The CPPA applies to a picture in a psychology manual, as well as a movie depicting the horrors of sexual abuse. It is not necessary, moreover, that the image be patently offensive. Pictures of what appear to be 17-year-olds engaging in sexually explicit activity do not in every case contravene community standards.

The CPPA prohibits speech despite its serious literary, artistic, political, or scientific value. The statute proscribes the visual depiction of an idea—that of teenagers engaging in sexual activity—that is a fact of modern society and has been a theme in art and literature throughout the ages. Under the CPPA, images are prohibited so long as the persons appear to be under 18 years of age. This is higher than the legal age for marriage in many States, as well as the age at which persons may consent to sexual relations. . . .

Both themes—teenage sexual activity and the sexual abuse of children—have inspired countless literary works. William Shakespeare created the most famous pair of teenage lovers, one of whom is just 13 years of age. See *Romeo and Juliet*, act I, sc. 2, 1.9 ("She hath not seen the change of fourteen years"). In the drama, Shakespeare portrays the relationship as something splendid and innocent, but not juvenile. The work has inspired no less than 40 motion pictures, some of which suggest that the teenagers consummated their relationship. Shakespeare may not have written sexually explicit scenes for the Elizabethan audience, but were modern directors to adopt a less conventional approach, that fact alone would not compel the conclusion that the work was obscene.

Contemporary movies pursue similar themes. Last year's Academy Awards featured the movie, *Traffic*, which was nominated for Best Picture. The film portrays a teenager, identified as a 16-year-old, who becomes addicted to drugs. The viewer sees the degradation of her addiction, which in the end leads her to a filthy room to trade sex for drugs. The year before, *American Beauty* won the Academy Award for Best Picture. In the course of the movie, a teenage girl engages in sexual relations with her teenage boyfriend, and another yields herself to the gratification of a middle-aged man. The film also contains a scene where, although the movie audience understands the act is not taking place, one character believes he is watching a teenage boy performing a sexual act on an older man.

Our society, like other cultures, has empathy and enduring fascination with the lives and destinies of the young. Art and literature express the vital interest we all have in the formative years we ourselves once knew, when wounds can be so grievous, disappointment so profound, and mistaken choices so tragic, but when moral acts and self-fulfillment are still in reach. Whether or not the films we mention violate the CPPA, they explore themes within the wide sweep of the statute's prohibitions. If these films, or hundreds of others of lesser note that explore those subjects, contain a single graphic depiction of sexual activity within the statutory definition, the possessor of the film would be subject to severe punishment without inquiry into the work's redeeming value. This is inconsistent with an essential First Amendment rule: The artistic merit of a work does not depend on the presence of a single explicit scene. Under *Miller*, the First Amendment requires that redeeming value be judged by considering the work as a whole. Where the scene is part of the narrative, the work itself does not for this reason become obscene, even though the scene in isolation might be offensive. For this reason, and the others we have noted, the CPPA cannot be read to prohibit obscenity, because it lacks the required link between its prohibitions and the affront to community standards prohibited by the definition of obscenity.

The Ban on Child Pornography Targets the Crime of Producing It

The Government seeks to address this deficiency by arguing that speech prohibited by the CPPA is virtually indistinguishable from child pornography, which may be banned without regard to whether it depicts works of value. Where the images are themselves the product of child sexual abuse, *Ferber* recognized that the State had an interest in stamping it out without regard to any judgment about its content. The production of the work, not its content, was the target of the statute. The fact that a work contained serious literary, artistic, or other value did not excuse the harm it caused to its child participants. . . .

Ferber upheld a prohibition on the distribution and sale of child pornography, as well as its production, because these acts were "intrinsically related" to the sexual abuse of children in two ways. First, as a permanent record of a child's abuse, the continued circulation itself would harm the child who had participated. Like a defamatory statement, each new publication of the speech would cause new injury to the child's reputation and emotional well-being. Second, because the traffic in child pornography was an economic motive for its production, the State had an interest in closing the distribution network. "The most expeditious if not the only practical method of law enforcement may be to dry up the market for this material by imposing severe criminal penalties on persons selling, advertising, or otherwise promoting the product." Under either rationale, the speech had what the Court in effect held was a proximate link to the crime from which it came. . . .

In contrast to the speech in *Ferber*, speech that itself is the record of sexual abuse, the CPPA prohibits speech that records no crime and creates no victims by its production. Virtual child pornography is not "intrinsically related" to the sexual abuse of children, as were the materials in *Ferber*. While the Government asserts that the images can lead to actual instances of child abuse, the causal link is contingent and indirect. The harm does not necessarily follow from the speech, but depends upon some unquantified potential for subsequent criminal acts. . . .

The CPPA, for reasons we have explored, is inconsistent with *Miller* and finds no support in *Ferber*. The Government seeks to justify its prohibitions in other ways. It argues that the CPPA is necessary because pedophiles may use virtual child pornography to seduce children. There are many things innocent in themselves, however, such as cartoons, video games, and candy, that might be used for immoral purposes, yet we would not expect those to be prohibited because they can be misused. The Government, of course, may punish adults who provide unsuitable materials to children, and it may enforce criminal penalties for unlawful solicitation. The precedents establish, however, that speech within the rights of adults to hear may not be silenced completely in an attempt to shield children from it. In *Butler v. Michigan*, the Court invalidated a statute prohibiting distribution of an indecent publication because of its tendency to "incite minors to violent or depraved or immoral acts." A unanimous Court agreed upon the important First Amendment principle that the State could not "reduce the adult population . . . to reading only what is fit for children.". . .

Speech That Might Encourage Illegal Conduct Cannot Be Banned

Here, the Government wants to keep speech from children not to protect them from its content but to protect them from those who would commit other crimes. The principle, however, remains the same: The Government cannot ban speech fit for adults simply because it may fall into the hands of children. The evil in question depends upon the actor's unlawful conduct, conduct defined as criminal quite apart from any link to the speech in question. This establishes that the speech ban is not narrowly drawn. The objective is to prohibit illegal conduct, but this restriction goes well beyond that interest by restricting the speech available to law-abiding adults.

The Government submits further that virtual child pornography whets the appetites of pedophiles and encourages them to engage in illegal conduct. This rationale cannot sustain the provision in question. The mere tendency of speech to encourage unlawful acts is not a sufficient reason for banning it. The government "cannot constitutionally premise legislation on the desirability of controlling a person's private thoughts." *Stanley v. Georgia.* First Amendment freedoms are most in danger when the government seeks to control thought or to justify its laws for that impermissible end. The right to think is the beginning of freedom, and speech must be protected from the government because speech is the beginning of thought.

To preserve these freedoms, and to protect speech for its own sake, the Court's First Amendment cases draw vital distinctions between words and deeds, between ideas and conduct. The government may not prohibit speech because it increases the chance an unlawful act will be committed "at some indefinite future time." *Hess v. Indiana.* The government may suppress speech for advocating the use of force or a violation of law only if "such advocacy is directed to inciting or producing imminent lawless action and is likely to incite or produce such action." *Brandenburg v. Ohio.* There is here no attempt, incitement, solicitation, or conspiracy. The Government has shown no more than a remote connection between speech that might encourage thoughts or impulses and any resulting child abuse. Without a significantly stronger, more direct connection, the Government may not prohibit speech on the ground that it may encourage pedophiles to engage in illegal conduct.

The Government next argues that its objective of eliminating the market for pornography produced using real children necessitates a prohibition on virtual images as well. Virtual images, the Government contends, are indistinguishable from real ones; they are part of the same market and are often exchanged. In this way, it is said, virtual images promote the trafficking in works produced through the exploitation of real children. The hypothesis is somewhat implausible. If virtual images were identical to illegal child pornography, the illegal images would be driven from the market by the indistinguishable substitutes. Few pornographers would risk prosecution by abusing real children if fictional, computerized images would suffice.

In the case of the material covered by *Ferber*, the creation of the speech is itself the crime of child abuse; the prohibition deters the crime by removing the profit motive . . . here, there is no underlying crime at all. Even it the Government's market deterrence theory were persuasive in some contexts, it would not justify this statute.

Lawful Speech Cannot Be Suppressed to Suppress Unlawful Speech

Finally, the Government says that the possibility of producing images by using computer imaging makes it very difficult for it to prosecute those who produce pornography by using real children. Experts, we are told, may have difficulty in saying whether the pictures were made by using real children or by using computer imaging. The necessary solution, the argument runs, is to prohibit both kinds of images. The argument, in essence, is that protected speech may be banned as a means to ban unprotected speech. This analysis turns the First Amendment upside down.

The Government may not suppress lawful speech as the means to suppress unlawful speech. Protected speech does not become unprotected merely because it resembles the latter. The Constitution requires the reverse. . . . The overbreadth doctrine prohibits the Government from banning unprotected speech if a substantial amount of protected speech is prohibited or chilled in the process.

To avoid the force of this objection, the Government would have us read the CPPA not as a measure suppressing speech but as a law shifting the burden to the accused to prove the speech is lawful. In this connection, the Government relies on an affirmative defense under the statute, which allows a defendant to avoid conviction for nonpossession offenses by showing that the materials were produced using only adults and were not otherwise distributed in a manner conveying the impression that they depicted real children. . . .

We need not decide, however, whether the Government could impose this burden on a speaker. Even if an affirmative defense can save a statute from First Amendment challenge, here the defense is incomplete and insufficient, even on its own terms. It allows persons to be convicted in some instances where they can prove children were not exploited in the production. A defendant charged with possessing, as opposed to distributing, proscribed works may not defend on the ground that the film depicts only adult actors. So while the affirmative defense may protect a movie producer from prosecution for the act of distribution, that same producer, and all other persons in the subsequent distribution chain, could be liable for possessing the prohibited work. Furthermore, the affirmative defense provides no protection to persons who produce speech by using computer imaging, or through other means that do not involve the use of adult actors who appear to be minors. In these cases, the defendant can demonstrate no children were harmed in producing the images, yet the affirmative defense would not bar the prosecution. For this reason, the affirmative defense cannot save the statute, for it leaves unprotected a substantial amount of speech not tied to the Government's interest in distinguishing images produced using real children from virtual ones.

In sum, Section 2256(8)(B) covers materials beyond the categories recognized in *Ferber* and *Miller*, and the reasons the Government offers in support of limiting the freedom of speech have no justification in our precedents or in the law of the First Amendment. The provision abridges the freedom to engage in a substantial amount of lawful speech. For this reason, it is overbroad and unconstitutional.

Respondents challenge Section 2256(8)(D) as well. This provision bans depictions of sexually explicit conduct that are "advertised, promoted, presented, described, or distributed in such a manner that conveys the impression that the material is or contains a visual depiction of a minor engaging in sexually explicit conduct.". . .

Even if a film contains no sexually explicit scenes involving minors, it could be treated as child pornography if the title and trailers convey the impression that the scenes would be found in the movie. The determination turns on how the speech is presented, not on what is depictcd....

The statute, furthermore, does not require that the context be part of an effort at "commercial exploitation." As a consequence, the CPPA does more than prohibit pandering. It prohibits possession of material described, or pandered, as child pornography by someone earlier in the distribution chain. The provision prohibits a sexually explicit film containing no youthful actors, just because it is placed in a box suggesting a prohibited movie. Possession is a crime even when the possessor knows the movie was mislabeled. The First Amendment requires a more precise restriction. For this reason, Section 2256(8)(D) is substantially overbroad and in violation of the First Amendment.

The judgment of the Court of Appeals is affirmed.

> "Other than computer generated images that are virtually indistinguishable from real children engaged in sexually explicitly conduct, the CPPA can be limited so as not to reach any material that was not already unprotected."

Dissenting Opinion: The Wording of CPPA Does Not Cover Any Material Protected by the First Amendment

William Rehnquist

William Rehnquist became a justice of the U.S. Supreme Court in 1972 and in 1986 President Ronald Reagan appointed him to be chief justice, a position he held until his death in 2005. He was a strong conservative and a supporter of states' rights, best known to the public for presiding over the impeachment trial of President Bill Clinton and for his role in Bush v. Gore, *the case that decided the 2000 presidential election. In his dissenting opinion in* Ashcroft v. Free Speech Coalition, *he argues that the Court should have upheld the Child Pornography Prevention Act (CPPA) because that act was not intended to cover movies with artistic value and its wording would not really apply to them. The mere suggestion of sexual activity by youthful-looking actors, he says, is not what Congress intended to ban with the word "simulated," and movie producers have not been interpreting the law that way during the time it has been in force. Fur-*

William Rehnquist, dissenting opinion, *John D. Ashcroft, Attorney General, et al., Petitioners v. The Free Speech Coalition et al*, U.S. Supreme Court, April 16, 2002.

thermore, such movies are not promoted as child pornography. So this issue should not prevent extension of the definition of child pornography to reach computer-generated images that are virtually indistinguishable from sexually explicit activity involving real children.

Congress has a compelling interest in ensuring the ability to enforce prohibitions of actual child pornography, and we should defer to its findings that rapidly advancing technology soon will make it all but impossible to do so. . . .

Serious First Amendment concerns would arise were the Government ever to prosecute someone for simple distribution or possession of a film with literary or artistic value, such as "Traffic" or "American Beauty.". . . The Child Pornography Prevention Act of 1996 (CPPA) need not be construed to reach such materials.

We normally do not strike down a statute on First Amendment grounds "when a limiting instruction has been or could be placed on the challenged statute." *Broadrick v. Oklahoma,* See, *e.g., New York v. Ferber,* (appreciating "the wide-reaching effects of striking down a statute on its face"); *Parker v. Levy,* ("This Court has . . . repeatedly expressed its reluctance to strike down a statute on its face where there were a substantial number of situations to which it might be validly applied"). This case should be treated no differently.

Other than computer generated images that are virtually indistinguishable from real children engaged in sexually explicitly conduct, the CPPA can be limited so as not to reach any material that was not already unprotected before the CPPA. The CPPA's definition of "sexually explicit conduct" is quite explicit in this regard. It makes clear that the statute only reaches "visual depictions" of:

> "[A]ctual or simulated . . . sexual intercourse, including genital-genital, oral-genital, anal-genital, or oral-anal, whether between persons of the same or opposite sex; . . .

bestiality; . . . masturbation; . . . sadistic or masochistic abuse; . . . or lascivious exhibition of the genitals or pubic area of any person."

The Court and Justice [Sandra Day] O'Connor suggest that this very graphic definition reaches the depiction of youthful looking adult actors engaged in suggestive sexual activity, presumably because the definition extends to "simulated" intercourse. Read as a whole, however, I think the definition reaches only the sort of "hard core of child pornography" that we found without protection in *Ferber.* So construed, the CPPA bans the visual depictions of youthful looking adult actors engaged in *actual* sexual activity; mere *suggestions* of sexual activity, such as youthful looking adult actors squirming under a blanket, are more akin to written descriptions than visual depictions, and thus fall outside the purview of the statute.

The CPPA Would Not Ban Romeo and Juliet

The reference to "simulated" has been part of the definition of "sexually explicit conduct" since the statute was first passed. See Protection of Children Against Sexual Exploitation Act of 1977. But the inclusion of "simulated" conduct, alongside "actual" conduct, does not change the "hard core" nature of the image banned. The reference to "simulated" conduct simply brings within the statute's reach depictions of hard core pornography that are "made to look genuine," Webster's Ninth New Collegiate Dictionary—including the main target of the CPPA, computer generated images virtually indistinguishable from real children engaged in sexually explicit conduct. Neither actual conduct nor simulated conduct, however, is properly construed to reach depictions such as those in a film portrayal of Romeo and Juliet, which are far removed from the hard core pornographic depictions that Congress intended to reach.

Indeed, we should be loath to construe a statute as banning film portrayals of Shakespearian tragedies, without some indication—from text or legislative history—that such a result was intended. In fact, Congress explicitly instructed that such a reading of the CPPA would be wholly unwarranted. As the Court of Appeals for the First Circuit has observed:

> "[T]he legislative record, which makes plain that the [CPPA] was intended to target only a narrow class of images—visual depictions 'which are virtually indistinguishable to unsuspecting viewers from unretouched photographs of actual children engaging in identical sexual conduct.'" *United States v. Hilton.*

Judge Ferguson similarly observed in his dissent in the Court of Appeals in this case:

> "From reading the legislative history, it becomes clear that the CPPA merely extends the existing prohibitions on 'real' child pornography to a narrow class of computer-generated pictures easily mistaken for real photographs of real children." *Free Speech Coalition v. Reno.*

See also [a committee report] ("[The CPPA] does not, and is not intended to, apply to a depiction produced using *adults* engaging i[n] sexually explicit conduct, even where a depicted individual may appear to be a minor" (emphasis in original)); ("[The CPPA] addresses the problem of 'high tech kiddie porn'"). We have looked to legislative history to limit the scope of child pornography statutes in the past, *United States v. X-Citement Video, Inc.*, and we should do so here as well.

This narrow reading of "sexually explicit conduct" not only accords with the text of the CPPA and the intentions of Congress; it is exactly how the phrase was understood prior to the broadening gloss the Court gives it today. Indeed, had "sexually explicit conduct" been thought to reach the sort of material the Court says it does, then films such as "Traffic" and "American Beauty" would not have been made the way they were. "Traffic" won its Academy Award in 2001. "American Beauty" won its Academy Award in 2000. But the CPPA has been on the books, and has been enforced, since 1996. The chill felt by the Court, ("[F]ew legitimate movie producers ... would risk distributing images in or near the uncertain reach of this law"), has apparently never been felt by those who actually make movies.

Prohibition Depends on How Material Is Promoted

To the extent the CPPA prohibits possession or distribution of materials that "convey the impression" of a child engaged in sexually explicit conduct, that prohibition can and should be limited to reach "the sordid business of pandering" which lies outside the bounds of First Amendment protection. *Ginzburg v. United States* (conduct that "deliberately emphasized the sexually provocative aspects of the work, in order to catch the salaciously disposed" may lose First Amendment protection). This is how the Government asks us to construe the statute, and it is the most plausible reading of the text, which prohibits only materials *"advertised, promoted, presented, described, or distributed in such a manner* that conveys the impression that the material is or contains a visual depiction of a minor engaging in sexually explicit conduct." (emphasis added).

The First Amendment may protect the video shopowner or film distributor who promotes material as "entertaining" or "acclaimed" regardless of whether the material contains depictions of youthful looking adult actors engaged in nonobscene but sexually suggestive conduct. The First Amendment does not, however, protect the panderer. Thus, materials promoted as conveying the impression that they depict actual minors engaged in sexually explicit conduct do not escape regulation merely because they might warrant First Amendment protection if promoted in a different manner. See *Ginzburg; Jacobellis v. Ohio*, (Warren, C.J., dissenting) ("In my opinion, the use to which various materials are put—not just the words and pictures themselves—must be considered in determining whether or not the materials are obscene"). I would construe "conveys the impression" as limited to the panderer, which makes the statute entirely consistent with *Ginzburg* and other cases.

The Court says that "conveys the impression" goes well beyond *Ginzburg* to "prohibi[t] [the] possession of material described, or pandered, as child pornography by someone earlier in the distribution chain." The Court's concern is that an individual who merely possesses protected materials (such as videocassettes of "Traffic" or "American Beauty") might offend the CPPA regardless of whether the individual actually intended to possess materials containing unprotected images. ("Individuals or businesses found to possess just three such films have no defense to criminal liability under the CPPA") (Justice O'Connor concurring in judgment in part and dissenting in part).

This concern is a legitimate one, but there is, again, no need or reason to construe the statute this way. In *X-Citement Video*, we faced a provision of the Protection of Children Against Sexual Exploitation Act of 1977, the precursor to the CPPA, which lent itself much less than the present statute to attributing a "knowingly" requirement to the contents of the possessed visual depictions. We held that such a requirement nonetheless applied, so that the Government would have to prove that a person charged with possessing child pornography actually knew that the materials contained depictions of real minors engaged in sexually explicit conduct. In light of this holding, and consistent with the narrow class of images the CPPA is intended to prohibit, the CPPA can be construed to prohibit only the knowing possession of materials actually containing visual depictions of real minors engaged in sexually explicit conduct, or computer generated images virtually indistinguishable from real minors engaged in sexually explicit

121

conduct. The mere possession of materials containing only suggestive depictions of youthful looking adult actors need not be so included.

In sum, while potentially impermissible applications of the CPPA may exist, I doubt that they would be "substantial . . . in relation to the statute's plainly legitimate sweep." *Broadrick.* The aim of ensuring the enforceability of our Nation's child pornography laws is a compelling one. The CPPA is targeted to this aim by extending the definition of child pornography to reach computer-generated images that are virtually indistinguishable from real children engaged in sexually explicit conduct. The statute need not be read to do any more than precisely this, which is not offensive to the First Amendment.

For these reasons, I would construe the CPPA in a manner consistent with the First Amendment, reverse the Court of Appeals' judgment, and uphold the statute in its entirety.

| "The Court's decision was not only cor-
rect, but will in the long run contribute
to the protection of children."

Allowing Speech Concerning Child Abuse Is More Likely to Remedy Abuse than Perpetuate It

Marci Hamilton

Marci A. Hamilton is a professor at Benjamin N. Cardozo School of Law, Yeshiva University. She is a columnist on constitutional issues for www.findlaw.com. In the following column, she argues that the Supreme Court was right to invalidate the Child Pornography Protection Act of 1996 (CPPA), which banned virtual child pornography that is produced without using real children. Those who criticize the decision, she says, have overlooked the value of art in helping society to deal with the evil of child abuse. Some fictional depictions of children engaged in sex are created by artists who are unsympathetic to the abusers, with the aim of bringing the topic into the open in order to protect children from predators. In Hamilton's opinion, censoring such images would do more harm than good.

Last week [April 2002] in *Ashcroft v. Free Speech Coalition*, the Supreme Court invalidated the Child Pornography Protection Act of 1996 (CPPA), which had prohibited purely fictional digital depictions of children engaged in sexual acts—

depictions that did not involve actual children. The Act's ban on "virtual" child pornography, the Court held, violated the First Amendment rights of adults.

The Court is now being unfairly lambasted for its decision. But critics need to take a deep breath and slow down.

I fully understand the motive behind the attacks on the Court—the laudable instinct to protect children. Yet the Court's decision was not only correct, but will in the long run contribute to the protection of children. Those criticizing the decision have elided the role and value of art in helping us to *deal* with the problems faced by children.

The Court's Decision May Aid in the Fight Against Child Abuse

The Court's decision recognizes a line between digital depictions of actual children engaged in sexual acts, and depictions of the same acts that do not involve actual children. The government, as the Court had previously held in *New York v. Ferber*, can constitutionally control the former. In this case, in contrast, the Court added that a broad and vague restriction on the latter chills adults' free speech.

Let us first all agree that depicting children having sex violates our collective sense of what is right. In addition, the government has carte blanche to ban "obscenity," under the standard set forth in *Miller v. California*, and to ban child pornography, under *Ferber*.

The problem for the critics of *Ashcroft v. Free Speech Coalition* is that the total suppression the government sought in the CPPA of non-obscene virtual images of child sexuality will not make our social ills—such as incest or abuse of children by trusted adults—go away. Indeed, a total ban like the CPPA makes it more difficult to constructively work out these demons.

For example, we are barely at the beginning of dealing with the monstrous actions taken by trusted and revered

Catholic priests. How will we come to terms with the abuse revealed in the recent scandal?

First, of course, there must be concrete steps taken to secure the safety of children—specifically, legal and church reform centered on protecting children from any future abuse. But assuming that the new structures are indeed put in place, what happens next? Do we blithely return to the path of contentment and relegate the topic of child abuse to the headlines of 2002?

No. It's too late for that. We must face those demons in order to vanquish them, and the motion pictures that inevitably will depict these tragedies offer us a low-cost, risk-free means of doing so. If an artist cannot depict the child being abused, she cannot accurately depict the monster who would abuse him. We will desperately need the opportunity art provides in order to more fully understand and, frankly, to fully condemn such actions.

Depictions of Child Abuse Can Be an Effective Way to Advocate Reform

Those criticizing the Court have the indisputably right moral instinct: to protect children from all harm. However, they do not serve children's interests well if they expect society simply to forgive and forget the harm that is inflicted on children on a regular basis in this society (and certainly not solely by the Catholic Church).

So long as real children are not used in the creation of works depicting child sexual acts, and real children are not exposed to these works once they are completed, the harm to children will be minimal—especially as compared to the harm to the adults' marketplace of ideas by censoring such images. In their rush to shield children, critics of the Court's recent decision forget that some depictions of children engaged in sex will be employed by artists whose viewpoint is sympathetic to the child and unsympathetic to the abuser, and these depictions will make the children's advocates' point far more forcefully and viscerally than a hundred dry brochures would have. In this case, a picture may be worth a thousand appeals for funds.

It has taken this culture a long time to begin to *protect* children from predators—in part because the topic was so taboo. We should not repeat the mistakes of the past and assume that because child sexual abuse itself is rightly anathema, discussion of it must also be anathema. Instead, let the topic be brought into the sunshine—where its ugly parameters can be accurately assessed, examined, and dealt with.

I hate the abuse of children, as do the members of the Court. But I welcome the artists who will help us to come to terms with our living nightmares, and I believe in their First Amendment right to include such materials in their artworks. As to which of these depictions I will choose to view, that is up to me, and to you. Let the market—not the government—determine that which is valuable in art and healing.

> *"There was, to put the matter bluntly, no good reason to throw free speech protections around pornography, nude dancing, raw profanity, and calls for law violation in the first place."*

Protection of Pornography Is Not Required by the First Amendment

Robert H. Bork

Robert H. Bork is a former U.S. solicitor general and federal Court of Appeals judge. He was nominated to the Supreme Court by President Ronald Reagan, but was not confirmed by the Senate. In the following viewpoint he argues that Supreme Court decisions on free speech issues have become increasingly permissive, to an extent not required by the Constitution. Ashcroft v. Free Speech Coalition, *in which the Court held that child pornography created without using real children cannot be outlawed, is merely the latest example. Until recently, Bork says, pornographers did not claim protection under the First Amendment, but now the precedents established by a succession of rulings have deprived the government of any effective sanctions. In his opinion, the Court should not deny society the power to set limits on speech of no social value.*

The Supreme Court is not testing the limits of free "speech" so much as it is obliterating them. The latest example is *Ashcroft v. Free Speech Coalition*, a decision holding that Congress may not prohibit child pornography created by using adults who look like minors or by using computer imaging. Justice Anthony Kennedy's majority opinion described the Child Pornography Prevention Act of 1996 as "proscrib[ing] a significant universe of speech" that fell "within the First Amendment's vast and privileged sphere." Since such speech was not "obscene" under the court's prior definition and did not involve real children in its production, the court found that the government had no constitutionally adequate grounds to suppress it.

To anyone unfamiliar with the court's extraordinarily permissive rulings in the past, it might seem that any depiction of children in a variety of sexual acts could be, and certainly should be, prohibited. The government, however, was limited by those rulings to arguing on grounds that virtually ensured its defeat.

To the suggestion that child pornography might be used to lure children into sexual encounters or might tip adults teetering on the verge of pedophilia over the line the court responded, "The prospect of crime . . . by itself does not justify laws suppressing protected speech."

The Case Sheds Light on the Direction of First Amendment Decisions

The importance of the *Free Speech Coalition* decision is less in its particular rejections of the government's necessarily limited rationales, however, than in the light the case throws upon the entire direction of First Amendment decisions that have brought the court to this point. There was, to put the matter bluntly, no good reason to throw free speech protections around pornography, nude dancing, raw profanity, and calls for law violation in the first place. Our jurisprudence has gone so far astray that there appears to be a right to display a picture of the Virgin Mary festooned with pornographic pictures and cow dung; but the presence of a crèche on government property is a forbidden establishment of religion under the same amendment.

There is nothing about the First Amendment that requires these results. That until relatively recently pornographers did not even raise the First Amendment in defending their sordid trade indicates how far we have come. It would seem merely common sense to think that graphic depictions of children in sexual acts would likely result in some action by pedophiles. The court finesses that problem with the statement that its "precedents establish . . . that speech within the rights of adults to hear may not be silenced completely in an attempt to shield children from it." Quite right. But why is pornography within the rights of adults to hear and see?

And why—to take only one category of speech undeserving of the court's solicitude—are the rawest forms of profanity exempt from regulation? Cable television is saturated with words never before used in public, and the broadcast networks are racing to catch up. The *New York Times* reports that in "A Season on the Brink," the character playing basketball coach Bobby Knight "drops the F-word 15 times in the first 15 minutes," and that the characters in "South Park" used a "well-known word for excrement 162 times in 30 minutes." The industry response to criticism on this score is that such words give the programs authenticity because this is the way people talk. In reality, however, the arrow probably points in the other direction.

People increasingly talk this way because they hear the words on television, and they hear the words on television because the Supreme Court's rulings have deprived the government of any effective sanctions for profanity. In justifying its decision here, the court actually said, "The right to think is the beginning of freedom, and speech must be protected from the government because speech is the beginning of thought." One wonders what valuable thoughts are triggered by child pornography or by nude dancing and profanity. The point is not that the court should outlaw such things; it has no power to do so. But it ought not to deny society the power to curb speech of no social value, indeed capable of inflicting great social harm.

There Is No Constitutional Justification for Destroying All Limits to Speech

In cases like *Free Speech Coalition*, the court, far from enhancing the value of thought, makes thought more difficult. The reduction of speech to the barracks-room level actively destroys thought that displays any subtlety, gradation or nuance. All that is protected is the right of the individual to satisfy his desires, no matter how base, without regard to the rights of others or the health of the society.

One justice who knows better justified his vote on these lines with the remark that too many precedents would have to be overturned in order to give the First Amendment its proper scope. That is certainly true, but the precedents that would have to be jettisoned were themselves innovations. There is no constitutional justification for a ratchet effect that progressively liberates the worst in our natures. By destroying limits to speech, the court severely handicaps the community's efforts to retain a morally and aesthetically satisfying environment.

"It is better to deny government the power to suppress that speech than it would be to allow it to suppress speech that may turn out to be valuable."

Unless All Speech Is Free, No Speech Is Free

Arnold H. Loewy

Arnold H. Loewy is a professor at Texas Tech University School of Law. In the following viewpoint he argues that the Supreme Court was right to invalidate the Child Pornography Protection Act (CPPA) provision that banned virtual child pornography, and that this was an important decision. Government should never be given the power to ban speech, he says, because ideas that are considered offensive in one era, such as speech about racial integration, may be recognized as valuable later on. Real child pornography is rightly suppressed not because it is abhorrent, but because it harms the children used in creating it. Loewy disagrees with the claim that virtual pornography encourages pedophiles or can be used to seduce children; he suggests that it may reduce the number of real children exploited in producing porn. In any case, in his opinion, one of the costs of free speech is recognition that speech may sometimes do more harm than good.

Although always believing that the United States Supreme Court should invalidate the Portion of the Child Pornography Protection Act (CPPA) that punishes the dissemination

Arnold H. Loewy, "Taking Free Speech Seriously: The United States Supreme Court and Virtual Child Pornography," *UNC Public Law Research Paper No. 02-17*, November 2002. Reproduced by permission of the publisher and author.

of images "that appear to be" a minor engaging in sexually-explicit conduct, I seriously doubted that it would do so. For one thing, the Court granted certiorari [agreed to review] in *Free Speech Coalition v. Reno*, a case in which the Ninth Circuit had *invalidated* the statute. Having previously denied certiorari in a case in which the lower courts had *upheld* the statute, there was good reason to believe that the Court intended to reverse the Ninth Circuit. Fortunately that didn't happen.

Apart from the procedural posture of the case, a cursory glance at the equities appears to favor the statute. The value of exploiting the sexuality of children certainly appears to be *de minimus*. Furthermore, the government made at least a surface case that virtual child pornography can be harmful to children. With that kind of a balance, one might have anticipated a willingness to accept the invitation of Judge Ferguson of the Ninth Circuit to create a new category of unprotected speech called "virtual child pornography." Though undoubtedly tempted, the Court rejected going down that wrong road. . . .

The Importance of Protecting Bad Speech

Few liberal democracies challenge freedom of speech in the abstract. Specific applications, however, are different. Many, who would never challenge freedom of speech in the abstract, balk at extending such protection to flag burners, and Nazis. Yet, the slightest reflection should reveal that unless all speech is free, no speech is free. No sensible government, including the most dictatorial, will ever prosecute good speech or even neutral speech. Indeed, no democracy would even think of prosecuting ordinarily bad speech (*e.g.* vote Republican). It is only when we get to very bad speech that the government even thinks about prosecution. Thus, it is in those situations in which free speech is needed most. Hence, protection for Nazis, flag burners, and virtual child pornographers logically follows if we want to take free speech seriously.

But should we want to take it seriously if the cost of doing so is to give added protection for speech that we would all be better off without? One's first intuition is to say "no," and indeed that is the result regularly reached in European courts and too frequently in American courts. The reason that this should bother us is that it gives government the power to decide which speech can compete in the marketplace and which speech is dead on arrival.

While some of us might be happy to relegate flag burning, Nazis, and virtual pornography to the scrapheap of dead on arrival speech, few would say that about speech urging racial integration. Yet speech urging racial integration fifty years ago would have been thought highly offensive to much of the citizenry of a large number of communities (including Charleston, South Carolina) and would have been subject to prohibition under a standard that protects the dignitary interest of some against the speech of others. Thus, even though government may be correct about some types of speech, it is better to deny government the power to suppress that speech than it would be to allow it to suppress speech that may turn out to be valuable (such as civil rights speech).

The fact that virtual pornography appears to be entertainment rather than ideological indoctrination is immaterial. In one of its most prescient moments, the Supreme Court of the United States observed:

> We do not accede to appellee's suggestion that the constitutional protection for a free press applies only to the exposition of ideas. The line between informing and entertaining is too elusive to draw (for the protection of that basic right). Everyone is familiar with instances of propaganda through fiction. What is one man's amusement teaches another's doctrine.

It is true that the United States Supreme Court exempts obscenity from its general relatively libertarian view of free speech, but as I have demonstrated elsewhere, this is more the result of fiat than logic. And, somewhat paradoxically, the concept of obscenity as unprotected speech is not the law in many European countries. In any event, the presence of the obscenity doctrine militates against, rather than for, a separate unprotected category of virtual child pornography. Given the American law of obscenity, which allows material that predominantly appeals to the prurient interest, describes sex in a patently offensive way, and lacks serious literary, artistic, political, and scientific value; to be prosecuted, the need for a special law condemning virtual child pornography is substantially reduced. Most really offensive virtual child pornography would likely be subject to prosecution as obscenity anyway, while a virtual sexually explicit presentation of Romeo and Juliet would not.

Distinguishing Real Child Pornography

Real child pornography is rightly subject to prosecution. But the reason that it is so treated has nothing to do with the abhorrent nature, or intrinsic worthlessness, of the material. It can be prosecuted for the same reason that employment of child labor can be prosecuted. Just as child labor harms the children that manufacture the goods to be sold, so does child pornography. It would not be a defense to a child labor prosecution that employment of children was necessary to enhance the quantity or quality of the product produced. Similarly, it should be no defense that the finished product had some kind of literary or artistic merit. It is the use of a child in an explicit sexual performance that is rightly forbidden.

Similarly, as the United States Supreme Court has suggested, morphed child pornography, that is images of a real child morphed to appear to be engaging in sexual activity, is enough like real child pornography that it should be treated as though it were real. A morphed image does not harm a real child by making the picture, but it does harm the child by providing an unauthorized permanent and false record of the child's engaging in sexual activity.

Apart from pornography that displays the image of a real child, actual or morphed, the objections to the material are similar to the objections to any kind of distasteful speech, and should be subject to the same kind of scrutiny. In the remainder of this paper, I shall explain why none of the justifications generally advanced against virtual child pornography warrant its prohibition.

Virtual Pornography's Capacity to Harm Real Children

Proponents of criminalizing virtual pornography argue that there are two ways in which the material can harm real children. First, they argue that virtual child pornography can whet a pedophile's appetite, making it more likely that he will abuse real children. Second, it is argued that a pedophile can use a picture of what appears to be a real child enjoying her sexuality as a visual aid to persuade an innocent victim to engage in similar activity. I will treat these arguments separately.

As to the first argument, I question both its factual accuracy and its legal significance. As to its accuracy, it is undoubtedly true that many, if not most, pedophiles possess child pornography. It is quite another thing to assume that the pornography caused the pedophilia. More likely, it was the perpetrator's attraction to children that caused him to possess the pornography rather than vice-versa. Indeed, one does not have to approach a "Clockwork Orange" scenario [a movie in which a criminal was shown images of violence and conditioned to find them sickening] to find behavioralists employing child pornography for the purpose of curing pedophiles.

I do not mean to argue that there has never been a pedophile who but for the pornography would not have committed his crime. But, that can hardly be the relevant standard. For one to sustain this justification, it would be necessary to establish that virtual child pornography (as opposed to real child pornography) has significantly increased pedophilia. To prove that five people who viewed virtual pornography committed an act of pedophilia that they otherwise would not have committed (assuming one could establish causation, which I doubt) would only tell half of the story. We would also have to know how many potential pedophiles had their appetites satiated by virtual child pornography, and therefore left real children alone.

To illustrate, three of the most heinous crimes in history were inspired respectively by the holy Bible, an Anglican High Church Service, and the movie the Ten Commandments. Obviously nobody measures the worth of these sources by the worst thing that they inspired. To be sure, child pornography, virtual or otherwise, has undoubtedly done far more harm and far less good than the aforementioned sources. Nevertheless, it is neither intuitively obvious, nor has it been proven, that eliminating all virtual pornography from the face of the earth would significantly reduce the incidents of pedophilia.

More importantly, even if it could be proven that virtual child pornography caused significant net harm, it would not follow that the law should permit its suppression. One of the costs of free speech is the recognition that sometimes speech will do more harm than good. Even so, for the reasons already given, it is better to allow it to cause whatever harm it may rather than allow the government the power to decide whether the book can be published at all. For example, [the novel] *The Turner Diaries* was said to have been the inspiration for Timothy McVeigh's massacre at Oklahoma City. It would not be hard for a court to conclude that on a cost/benefit basis that book should be condemned. Indeed, it is hard for me to believe that *The Turner Diaries* did not do significantly more harm than good. Yet, I would vehemently oppose the government's power to remove it from the marketplace of ideas.

To further illustrate the wrongness of allowing judges (or legislators) to condemn a book based on its net harm, imagine a claim in the United States that the Qur'an should be banned because it was said to inspire the 9/11 terrorists. Would anybody feel comfortable leaving a good versus harm standard to American judges, most of whom are Christian, in regard to Islam's holiest book? I certainly would not, and thus conclude that even if virtual child pornography were conclusively shown to do more harm than good, the Supreme Court was correct in not allowing it to be eliminated.

As to the argument that virtual pornography can be used to seduce children, Justice Kennedy, for the Supreme Court, got it exactly right when he noted that if virtual pornography is to be suppressed because of its capacity to seduce children, we might as well suppress "cartoons, video games, and candy." And, I might add that he could have included bicycles, puppy dogs, and vans. The point, of course, is that many things, including but not limited to literature, can be misused. But, as the Court once succinctly put it: "We cannot reduce the entire adult population to reading only that which is fit for children."

Distinguishing Virtual from Real Child Pornography

By far the most powerful argument for punishing virtual child pornography is the difficulty of distinguishing it from the real thing. The argument is that virtual and real pictures look so indistinguishable that a person marketing real child pornography might argue either that the material is virtual (and you can't prove beyond a reasonable doubt that it isn't) or at least that the defendant believed that it was virtual. To the extent that this argument rests on a factually sound premise, it presents a very serious problem. If real child pornography is punishable, but virtual isn't, and you can't tell the difference, what's a government to do?

The good news is that, at least for now, that does not seem to be an insurmountable problem. Although defendants have argued that the material was virtual, it has never been a successful defense. Furthermore, there is technology available that allows the government to take a picture apart, pixel by pixel, to determine its origin. Thus, as with the erstwhile nuclear arms race, detection appears to be keeping up with technology.

To the extent that technology outstrips detection and one really cannot tell the difference, some type of burden of proof shifting device might be appropriate. Surely, the government should be able to argue that a picture that appears real can be treated as real in the absence of evidence that it isn't. Such a rule would differ from the one at issue in *Ashcroft*, where the statute allowed punishment even when it was clear that the picture was virtual.

As for the *scienter* issue [whether the defendant knowingly did wrong], presumably it would take more than the defendant's word that he intended to transmit virtual pictures to create a reasonable doubt. If the Government proves that the pictures are real, a simple statement from the defendant that he thought they were virtual would be very unlikely to create a reasonable doubt.

Decriminalizing Virtual Pornography May Protect Real Children

It is certainly not immediately obvious that real children would be *better* off by allowing the sale of virtual pornography, yet that may in fact be the case. In an ideal world, nobody would want child pornography, real or virtual. Unfortunately, the world we live in is not ideal. Despite the efforts of all civilized governments to suppress child pornography, it is still with us. Why? Simply because the demand is there. If one accepts the unfortunate truth that the demand for child pornography exists despite these governmental efforts, there is little reason to believe that we will totally stamp it out.

On the other hand, if virtual child pornography is (or can be made) nearly identical to real child pornography and only the latter is unlawful, why wouldn't the pornographer sell only the former? Certainly most pornographers would love to avoid the risk of prison if their anticipated profit would not be compromised. And from the consumer's perspective, a virtual picture would also shield him from prosecution: Thus, there is good reason to believe that legalizing virtual child pornography may reduce the number of children that are currently exploited by this perverted industry. And so, the United states Supreme Court may well have rendered a decision that will ultimately protect children as well as it protects freedom of speech.

CHAPTER 4

CHAPTER 4

Schools May Suppress Student Speech That Advocates Use of Illegal Drugs

Case Overview

Deborah Morse et al. v. Joseph Frederick (2007)

In January of 2002 the Olympic Torch was carried through the streets of Juneau, Alaska, on its way to the Winter Games. The parade passed by the high school, and students were let out of class to watch. Whether this was an official "school event" has been debated; the band and cheerleaders participated and teachers were present, but the parade was sponsored by Coca-Cola, not the school, and attendance was not compulsory. Some of the students threw snowballs and plastic soda bottles or got into fights. Eighteen-year-old senior Joseph Frederick, however, had a different idea. To attract TV news cameras, he unfurled a 15-foot banner with the words "Bong Hits 4 Jesus," which he later said were designed to be meaningless and funny. It is unlikely that he suspected these words would ultimately be headlined in newspapers and magazines throughout the nation.

When high school principal Deborah Morse saw Frederick's banner, she told him to take it down even though it was not on school premises. He refused, so she tore it down herself and suspended him from school for ten days. Frederick appealed unsuccessfully to the school board, then filed suit in federal court on grounds that his First Amendment right to free speech had been violated. The District Court ruled that there had been no violation and that in any case the principal was immune from suit—in other words, could not be sued for money—because she had believed she was doing her job. Frederick's lawyer then appealed the case to the Circuit Court, which not only ruled in his favor, but declared that Deborah Morse should have known she was violating his constitutional rights and therefore was not immune from being personally sued. With the backing of the school board and a number of powerful organizations, she took her case to the U.S. Supreme Court.

The Supreme Court accepts only a fraction of the cases that are appealed to it, and observers were surprised when it agreed to review this one. Many thought that a mere prank was too trivial an incident to waste the Court's time on. Others felt that free speech had been so clearly suppressed that appeal was pointless. However, much more was involved. Deborah Morse and her supporters viewed the case as being about illegal drugs. "Bong hits" is a reference to marijuana, and Morse maintained that she tore down the banner because she felt it undermined the school's "mission" to oppose drug use; also she feared the public would take its display to mean that the school condoned it. Although Frederick said he hadn't intended any advocacy of drugs, his attorneys pointed out that legalization of marijuana has been a political issue in Alaska and student political speech is fully protected under the *Tinker* standard. Large national organizations opposed to drug use, and even the U.S. government, entered the fray; by the time it got to the Supreme Court, the argument centered on whether or not the schools have a basic responsibility to discourage illegal drugs at the cost of censoring speech.

There were additional issues. Educators were dismayed by a legal precedent that would allow well-intentioned administrators to be personally sued for money when they did what they believed was right. Also, people on both sides of the free speech debate were concerned about the question of how much control schools are permitted to have over off-campus speech; some said the Supreme Court's decision could affect whether schools can discipline students for what they post online. And while conservative anti-drug organizations supported Morse, several large conservative religious organizations filed amicus (friend of the court) briefs supporting Frederick because they feared that a ruling against him would give schools authority to censor speech they found inconsistent with any position they wanted to define as part of their educational mission, and thus might restrict religious freedom.

"The most important student free-speech conflict to reach the Supreme Court since the height of the Vietnam War hinges on a somewhat absurd, vaguely offensive, mostly nonsensical message of protest," said the *Washington Post*. The Court ruled in favor of Morse, holding that schools may prohibit speech that appears to advocate illegal drug use. However, two justices stated in a concurring opinion that they had joined the majority only with the understanding that the decision "provides no support for any restriction of speech that can be plausibly interpreted as commenting on any political or social issue." Three other justices strongly disagreed with the decision and joined in a dissenting opinion, deploring the fact that, "Although this case began with a silly, nonsensical banner, it ends with the Court inventing out of whole cloth a special First Amendment rule permitting the censorship of any student speech that mentions drugs."

The Court's Decision: The First Amendment Does Not Require Schools to Tolerate Encouragement of Drug Use

John Roberts

John Roberts became chief justice of the Supreme Court in September 2005, the third-youngest person who has ever held that position as well as the Court's youngest member. He was previously a judge on the U.S. Court of Appeals and before that, in his private law practice, he argued many cases before the Supreme Court. He now heads its conservative majority, although in some cases he has sided with liberals. In Morse v. Frederick, he wrote the majority opinion, which held that school principal Deborah Morse was not violating the First Amendment when she disciplined Joseph Frederick for displaying a banner with the words "Bong Hits 4 Jesus" at a school event. The majority of the Court felt that her interpretation of the banner as promotion of illegal drug use was reasonable, and that because Frederick's message was not political speech that advocated a change in the law, its suppression by the school was permissible.

A t a school-sanctioned and school-supervised event, a high school principal saw some of her students unfurl a large banner conveying a message she reasonably regarded as pro-

John Roberts, majority opinion, *Deborah Morse, et al., Petitioners v. Joseph Frederick*, U.S. Supreme Court, June 25, 2007.

moting illegal drug use. Consistent with established school policy prohibiting such messages at school events, the principal directed the students to take down the banner. One student—among those who had brought the banner to the event—refused to do so. The principal confiscated the banner and later suspended the student. The Ninth Circuit held that the principal's actions violated the First Amendment, and that the student could sue the principal for damages.

Our cases make clear that students do not "shed their constitutional rights to freedom of speech or expression at the schoolhouse gate." [See Chapter 1 of this book.] *Tinker v. Des Moines Independent Community School Dist.* At the same time, we have held that "the constitutional rights of students in public school are not automatically coextensive with the rights of adults in other settings," *Bethel School Dist. No. 403 v. Fraser*, and that the rights of students "must be 'applied in light of the special characteristics of the school environment.'" *Hazelwood School Dist. v. Kuhlmeir*, [See Chapter 2 of this book] (quoting *Tinker*). Consistent with these principles, we hold that schools may take steps to safeguard those entrusted to their care from speech that can reasonably be regarded as encouraging illegal drug use. We conclude that the school officials in this case did not violate the First Amendment by confiscating the pro-drug banner and suspending the student responsible for it. . . .

We granted certiorari [review] on two questions: whether Frederick had a First Amendment right to wield his banner, and, if so, whether that right was so clearly established that the principal may be held liable for damages. We resolve the first question against Frederick, and therefore have no occasion to reach the second.

At the outset, we reject Frederick's argument that this is not a school speech case—as has every other authority to address the question. The event occurred during normal school hours. It was sanctioned by Principal Morse "as an approved

social event or class trip," and the school district's rules expressly provide that pupils in "approved social events and class
trips are subject to district rules for student conduct." Teachers and administrators were interspersed among the students
and charged with supervising them. The high school band
and cheerleaders performed. Frederick, standing among other
JDHS [Juneau-Douglas High School] students across the street
from the school, directed his banner toward the school, making it plainly visible to most students. Under these circumstances, we agree with the superintendent that Frederick cannot "stand in the midst of his fellow students, during school
hours, at a school-sanctioned activity and claim he is not at
school." There is some uncertainty at the outer boundaries as
to when courts should apply school-speech precedents, but
not on these facts.

The message on Frederick's banner is cryptic. It is no
doubt offensive to some, perhaps amusing to others. To still
others, it probably means nothing at all. Frederick himself
claimed "that the words were just nonsense meant to attract
television cameras." But Principal Morse thought the banner
would be interpreted by those viewing it as promoting illegal
drug use, and that interpretation is plainly a reasonable one.

As Morse later explained in a declaration, when she saw
the sign, she thought that "the reference to a 'bong hit' would
be widely understood by high school students and others as
referring to smoking marijuana." She further believed that
"display of the banner would be construed by students, District personnel, parents and others witnessing the display of
the banner, as advocating or promoting illegal drug use"—in
violation of school policy. . . .

We agree with Morse. At least two interpretations of the
words on the banner demonstrate that the sign advocated the
use of illegal drugs. First, the phrase could be interpreted as
an imperative: "[Take] bong hits . . ."—a message equivalent,
as Morse explained in her declaration, to "smoke marijuana"

or "use an illegal drug." Alternatively, the phrase could be viewed as celebrating drug use—"bong hits [are a good thing]," or "[we take] bong hits"—and we discern no meaningful distinction between celebrating illegal drug use in the midst of fellow students and outright advocacy or promotion. . . .

The pro-drug interpretation of the banner gains further plausibility given the paucity of alternative meanings the banner might bear. The best Frederick can come up with is that the banner is "meaningless and funny.". . . Gibberish is surely a possible interpretation of the words on the banner, but it is not the only one, and dismissing the banner as meaningless ignores its undeniable reference to illegal drugs.

The dissent mentions Frederick's "credible and uncontradicted explanation for the message—he just wanted to get on television." But that is a description of Frederick's *motive* for displaying the banner; it is not an interpretation of what the banner says. The *way* Frederick was going to fulfill his ambition of appearing on television was by unfurling a pro-drug banner at a school event, in the presence of teachers and fellow students.

Elsewhere in its opinion, the dissent emphasizes the importance of political speech and the need to foster "national debate about a serious issue," as if to suggest that the banner is political speech. But not even Frederick argues that the banner conveys any sort of political or religious message. Contrary to the dissent's suggestion, this is plainly not a case about political debate over the criminalization of drug use or possession.

The question thus becomes whether a principal may, consistent with the First Amendment, restrict student speech at a school event, when that speech is reasonably viewed as promoting illegal drug use. We hold that she may. . . .

Tinker held that student expression may not be suppressed unless school officials reasonably conclude that it will "materially and substantially disrupt the work and discipline of the school." The essential facts of *Tinker* are quite stark, implicating concerns at the heart of the First Amendment. The students sought to engage in political speech, using the armbands to express their "disapproval of the Vietnam hostilities and their advocacy of a truce, to make their views known, and, by their example, to influence others to adopt them." Political speech, of course, is "at the core of what the First Amendment is designed to protect." *Virginia v. Black.* The only interest the Court discerned underlying the school's actions was the "mere desire to avoid the discomfort and unpleasantness that always accompany an unpopular viewpoint," or "an urgent wish to avoid the controversy which might result from the expression." *Tinker.* That interest was not enough to justify banning "a silent, passive expression of opinion, unaccompanied by any disorder or disturbance."

This Court's next student speech case was *Fraser*, Matthew Fraser was suspended for delivering a speech before a high school assembly in which he employed what this Court called "an elaborate, graphic, and explicit sexual metaphor." Analyzing the case under *Tinker*, the District Court and Court of Appeals found no disruption, and therefore no basis for disciplining Fraser. This Court reversed, holding that the "School District acted entirely within its permissible authority in imposing sanctions upon Fraser in response to his offensively lewd and indecent speech."

The mode of analysis employed in *Fraser* is not entirely clear. The Court was plainly attuned to the content of Fraser's speech, citing the "marked distinction between the political 'message' of the armbands in *Tinker* and the sexual content of [Fraser's] speech." But the Court also reasoned that school boards have the authority to determine "what manner of speech in the classroom or in school assembly is inappropriate." . . .

We need not resolve this debate to decide this case. For present purposes, it is enough to distill from *Fraser* two basic principles. First, *Fraser's* holding demonstrates that "the constitutional rights of students in public school are not automatically coextensive with the rights of adults in other settings." Had Fraser delivered the same speech in a public forum outside the school context, it would have been protected. In school, however, Fraser's First Amendment rights were circumscribed in "light of the special characteristics of the school environment." Second, *Fraser* established that the mode of analysis set forth in *Tinker* is not absolute. Whatever approach *Fraser* employed, it certainly did not conduct "substantial disruption" analysis prescribed by *Tinker*. . . .

Our most recent student speech case, *Kuhlmeier*, concerned "expressive activities that students, parents, and members of the public might reasonably perceive to bear the imprimatur of the school." Staff members of a high school newspaper sued their school when it chose not to publish two of their articles. The Court of Appeals analyzed the case, under *Tinker*, ruling in favor of the students because it found no evidence of material disruption to classwork or school discipline. This Court reversed, holding that "educators do not offend the First Amendment by exercising editorial control over the style and content of student speech in school-sponsored expressive activities so long as their actions are reasonably related to legitimate pedagogical concerns."

Kuhlmeier does not control this case because no one would reasonably believe that Frederick's banner bore the school's imprimatur. The case is nevertheless instructive because it confirms both principles cited above. *Kuhlmeier* acknowledged that schools may regulate some speech "even though the government could not censor similar speech outside the school." And, like *Fraser*, it confirms that the rule of *Tinker* is not the only basis for restricting student speech.

Drawing on the principles applied in our student speech cases, we have held in the Fourth Amendment context that "while children assuredly do not 'shed their constitutional rights . . . at the schoolhouse gate,' . . . the nature of those rights is what is appropriate for children in school." *Vernonia School Dist. 47J v. Acton*, (quoting *Tinker*). In particular, "the school setting requires some easing of the restrictions to which searches by public authorities are ordinarily subject." *New Jersey v. T. L. O.* . . .

Even more to the point, these cases also recognize that deterring drug use by schoolchildren is an "important—indeed, perhaps compelling" interest. Drug abuse can cause severe and permanent damage to the health and well-being of young people. . . .

Congress has declared that part of a school's job is educating students about the dangers of illegal drug use. It has provided billions of dollars to support state and local drug-prevention program. . . .

Thousands of school boards throughout the country—including JDHS—have adopted policies aimed at effectuating this message. Those school boards know that peer pressure is perhaps "the single most important factor leading schoolchildren to take drugs," and that students are more likely to use drugs when the norms in school appear to tolerate such behavior. *Earls.* Student speech celebrating illegal drug use at a school event, in the presence of school administrators and teachers, thus poses a particular challenge for school officials working to protect those entrusted to their care from the dangers of drug abuse.

The "special characteristics of the school environment," *Tinker*, and the governmental interest in stopping student drug abuse—reflected in the policies of Congress and myriad school boards, including JDHS—allow schools to restrict student expression that they reasonably regard as promoting illegal drug use. *Tinker* warned that schools may not prohibit student speech because of "undifferentiated fear or apprehension of disturbance" or "a mere desire to avoid the discomfort and unpleasantness that always accompany an unpopular viewpoint." The danger here is far more serious and palpable. The particular concern to prevent student drug abuse at issue here, embodied in established school policy, extends well beyond an abstract desire to avoid controversy.

Petitioners urge us to adopt the broader rule that Frederick's speech is proscribable because it is plainly "offensive" as that term is used in *Fraser*. We think this stretches *Fraser* too far; that case should not be read to encompass any speech that could fit under some definition of "offensive." After all, much political and religious speech might be perceived as offensive to some. The concern here is not that Frederick's speech was offensive, but that it was reasonably viewed as promoting illegal drug use. . . .

Even the dissent recognizes that the issues here are close enough that the principal should not be held liable in damages, but should instead enjoy qualified immunity for her actions. Stripped of rhetorical flourishes, then, the debate between the dissent and this opinion is less about constitutional first principles than about whether Frederick's banner constitutes promotion of illegal drug use. We have explained our view that it does. The dissent's contrary view on that relatively narrow question hardly justifies sounding the First Amendment bugle.

School principals have a difficult job, and a vitally important one. When Frederick suddenly and unexpectedly unfurled his banner, Morse had to decide to act—or not act—on the spot. It was reasonable for her to conclude that the banner promoted illegal drug use—in violation of established school policy—and that failing to act would send a powerful message to the students in her charge, including Frederick, about how serious the school was about the dangers of illegal drug use.

The First Amendment does not require schools to tolerate at school events student expression that contributes to those dangers.

> "Carving out pro-drug speech for uniquely harsh treatment finds no support in our case law and is inimical to the values protected by the First Amendment."

Dissenting Opinion: Students Should Not Be Punished for Speech with Which Schools Disagree

John Paul Stevens

John Paul Stevens is the oldest and longest-serving justice of the Supreme Court, having taken his seat in 1975 after serving as a judge of the U.S. Court of Appeals. Although he was appointed to the Court by a Republican president, he has sided with its liberal members on many issues. The following selection is his dissenting opinion in Morse v. Frederick, *in which he was joined by Justices David Souter and Ruth Bader Ginsburg. In it he argues that the Court was mistaken in upholding the school's decision to punish Frederick for displaying a banner that was not intended to advocate illegal conduct and was unlikely to provoke it. Free speech should not be suppressed simply because society disagrees with its content. "In the national debate about a serious issue," Justice Stevens says, "it is the expression of the minority's viewpoint that most demands the protection of the First Amendment."*

John Paul Stevens, dissenting opinion, *Deborah Morse, et al., Petitioners v. Joseph Frederick*, U.S. Supreme Court, June 25, 2007.

A significant fact barely mentioned by the Court sheds a revelatory light on the motives of both the students and the principal of Juneau-Douglas High School (JDHS). On January 24, 2002, the Olympic Torch Relay gave those Alaska residents a rare chance to appear on national television. As Joseph Frederick repeatedly explained, he did not address the curious message—"BONG HiTS 4 JESUS"—to his fellow students. He just wanted to get the camera crews' attention. Moreover, concern about a nationwide evaluation of the conduct of the JDHS student body would have justified the principal's decision to remove an attention-grabbing 14-foot banner, even if it had merely proclaimed "Glaciers Melt!"

I agree with the Court that the principal should not be held liable for pulling down Frederick's banner. I would hold, however, that the school's interest in protecting its students from exposure to speech "reasonably regarded as promoting illegal drug use," cannot justify disciplining Frederick for his attempt to make an ambiguous statement to a television audience simply because it contained an oblique reference to drugs. The First Amendment demands more, indeed, much more.

The Court holds otherwise only after laboring to establish two uncontroversial propositions: first, that the constitutional rights of students in school settings are not coextensive with the rights of adults, and second, that deterring drug use by schoolchildren is a valid and terribly important interest. As to the first, I take the Court's point that the message on Frederick's banner is not *necessarily* protected speech, even though it unquestionably would have been had the banner been unfurled elsewhere. As to the second, I am willing to assume that the Court is correct that the pressing need to deter drug use supports JDHS's rule prohibiting willful conduct that expressly "advocates the use of substances that are illegal to minors." But it is a gross non sequitur to draw from these two unremarkable propositions the remarkable conclusion that the school may suppress student speech that was never meant to persuade anyone to do anything.

In my judgment, the First Amendment protects student speech if the message itself neither violates a permissible rule nor expressly advocates conduct that is illegal and harmful to students. This nonsense banner does neither, and the Court does serious violence to the First Amendment in upholding—indeed, lauding—a school's decision to punish Frederick for expressing a view with which it disagreed.

In December 1965, we were engaged in a controversial war, a war that "divided this country as few other issues ever have." *Tinker v. Des Moines*. Having learned that some students planned to wear black armbands as a symbol of opposition to the country's involvement in Vietnam, officials of the Des Moines public school district adopted a policy calling for the suspension of any student who refused to remove the armband. As we explained when we considered the propriety of that policy, "[t]he school officials banned and sought to punish petitioners for a silent, passive expression of opinion, unaccompanied by any disorder or disturbance on the part of petitioners." The district justified its censorship on the ground that it feared that the expression of a controversial and unpopular opinion would generate disturbances. Because the school officials had insufficient reason to believe that those disturbances would "materially and substantially interfere with the requirements of discipline in the operation of the school," we found the justification for the rule to lack any foundation and therefore held that the censorship violated the First Amendment.

Justice Harlan dissented, but not because he thought the school district could censor a message with which it disagreed. Rather, he would have upheld the district's rule only because the students never cast doubt on the district's anti-disruption justification by proving that the rule was motivated "by other than legitimate school concerns—for example, a desire to prohibit the expression of an unpopular point of view while permitting expression of the dominant opinion."

Two cardinal First Amendment principles animate both the Court's opinion in *Tinker* and Justice Harlan's dissent. First, censorship based on the content of speech, particularly censorship that depends on the viewpoint of the speaker, is subject to the most rigorous burden of justification. . . .

Second, punishing someone for advocating illegal conduct is constitutional only when the advocacy is likely to provoke the harm that the government seeks to avoid. . . .

However necessary it may be to modify those principles in the school setting, *Tinker* affirmed their continuing vitality. . . .

As other federal courts have long recognized, under *Tinker*,

> "regulation of student speech is generally permissible only when the speech would substantially disrupt or interfere with the work of the school or the rights of other students. . . . *Tinker* requires a specific and significant fear of disruption, *not just some remote apprehension of disturbance.*" *Saxe v. State College Area School Dist.*, (emphasis added).

Yet today the Court fashions a test trivializes the two cardinal principles upon which *Tinker* rests. The Court's test invites stark viewpoint discrimination. In this case, for example, the principal has unabashedly acknowledged that she disciplined Frederick because she disagreed with the pro-drug viewpoint she ascribed to the message on the banner,—a viewpoint, incidentally that Frederick has disavowed . . . . the Court's holding in this case strikes at "the heart of the First Amendment" because it upholds a punishment meted out on the basis of a listener's disagreement with her understanding (or, more likely, misunderstanding) of the speaker's viewpoint. "If there is a bedrock principle underlying the First Amendment, it is that the Government may not prohibit the expression of an idea simply because society finds the idea itself offensive or disagreeable." *Texas v. Johnson.*

It is also perfectly clear that "promoting illegal drug use," comes nowhere close to proscribable "incitement to imminent lawless action." *Brandenburg*, 395 U. S., at 447. Encouraging drug use might well increase the likelihood that a listener will try an illegal drug, but that hardly justifies censorship:

> "Every denunciation of existing law tends in some measure to increase the probability that there will be violation of it. Condonation of a breach enhances the probability. Expressions of approval add to the probability. . . . Advocacy of law-breaking heightens it still further. But even advocacy of violation, however reprehensible morally, is not a justification for denying free speech where the advocacy falls short of incitement and there is nothing to indicate that the advocacy would be immediately acted upon." *Whitney v. California.*

No one seriously maintains that drug advocacy (much less Frederick's ridiculous sign) comes within the vanishingly small category of speech that can be prohibited because of its feared consequences. Such advocacy, to borrow from Justice Holmes, "ha[s] no chance of starting a present conflagration." *Gitlow v. New York.*

The Court rejects outright these twin foundations of *Tinker* because, in its view, the unusual importance of protecting children from the scourge of drugs supports a ban on all speech in the school environment that promotes drug use. Whether or not such a rule is sensible as a matter of policy, carving out pro-drug speech for uniquely harsh treatment finds no support in our case law and is inimical to the values protected by the First Amendment.

I will nevertheless assume for the sake of argument that the school's concededly powerful interest in protecting its students adequately supports its restriction on "any assembly or public expression that . . . advocates the use of substances that are illegal to minors. . . ." Given that the relationship between schools and students "is custodial and tutelary, permitting a degree of supervision and control that could not be exercised over free adults," *Vernonia School Dist. 47J v. Acton*, 515 U. S. 646, 655 (1995), it might well be appropriate to tolerate some targeted viewpoint discrimination in this unique setting. And while conventional speech may be restricted only when likely to "incit[e] imminent lawless action," *Brandenburg*, it is possible that our rigid imminence requirement ought to be relaxed at schools. . . .

But it is one thing to restrict speech that *advocates* drug use. It is another thing entirely to prohibit an obscure message with a drug theme that a third party subjectively—and not very reasonably—thinks is tantamount to express advocacy. . . . Even the school recognizes the paramount need to hold the line between, on the one hand, non-disruptive speech that merely expresses a viewpoint that is unpopular or contrary to the school's preferred message, and on the other hand, advocacy of an illegal or unsafe course of conduct. The district's prohibition of drug advocacy is a gloss on a more general rule that is otherwise quite tolerant of non-disruptive student speech. . . .

There is absolutely no evidence that Frederick's banner's reference to drug paraphernalia "willful[ly]" infringed on anyone's rights or interfered with any of the school's educational programs. . . . Therefore, just as we insisted in *Tinker* that the school establish some likely connection between the armbands and their feared consequences, so too JDHS must show that Frederick's supposed advocacy stands a meaningful chance of making otherwise-abstemious students try marijuana.

But instead of demanding that the school make such a showing, the Court punts. Figuring out just *how* it punts is tricky. . . . On occasion, the Court suggests it is deferring to the principal's "reasonable" judgment that Frederick's sign qualified as drug advocacy. At other times, the Court seems to say that *it* thinks the banner's message constitutes express advocacy. Either way, its approach is indefensible.

To the extent the Court defers to the principal's ostensibly reasonable judgment, it abdicates its constitutional responsibility. The beliefs of third parties, reasonable or otherwise, have never dictated which messages amount to proscribable advocacy. Indeed, it would be a strange constitutional doctrine that would allow the prohibition of only the narrowest category of speech advocating unlawful conduct, yet would permit a listener's perceptions to determine which speech deserved constitutional protection. . . .

To the extent the Court independently finds that "BONG HiTS 4 JESUS" *objectively* amounts to the advocacy of illegal drug use—in other words, that it can *most* reasonably be interpreted as such—that conclusion practically refutes itself. This is a nonsense message, not advocacy. The Court's feeble effort to divine its hidden meaning is strong evidence of that. . . .

Frederick's credible and uncontradicted explanation for the message—he just wanted to get on television—is also relevant because a speaker who does not intend to persuade his audience can hardly be said to be advocating anything. But most importantly, it takes real imagination to read a "cryptic" message (the Court's characterization, not mine, with a slanting drug reference as an incitement to drug use. Admittedly, some high school students (including those who use drugs) are dumb. Most students, however, do not shed their brains at the schoolhouse gate, and most students know dumb advocacy when they see it. The notion that the message on this banner would actually persuade either the average student or even the dumbest one to change his or her behavior is most implausible. That the Court believes such a silly message can be proscribed as advocacy underscores the novelty of its position, and suggests that the principle it articulates has no stopping point.

Even if advocacy could somehow be wedged into Frederick's obtuse reference to marijuana, that advocacy was at best subtle and ambiguous. There is abundant precedent, . . . for the proposition that when the "First Amendment is implicated, the tie goes to the speaker," *Federal Election Comm'n v. Winconsin Right to Life,* and that "when it comes to defining what speech qualifies as the functional equivalent of express advocacy . . . we give the benefit of the doubt to speech, not censorship." If this were a close case, the tie would have to go to Frederick's speech, not to the principal's strained reading of his quixotic message.

Among other things, the Court's ham-handed, categorical approach is deaf to the constitutional imperative to permit unfettered debate, even among high-school students, about the wisdom of the war on drugs or of legalizing marijuana for medicinal use. See *Tinker,* "[Students] may not be confined to the expression of those sentiments that are officially approved"). If Frederick's stupid reference to marijuana can in the Court's view justify censorship, then high school students everywhere could be forgiven for zipping their mouths about drugs at school lest some "reasonable" observer censor and then punish them for promoting drugs.

Consider, too, that the school district's rule draws no distinction between alcohol and marijuana, but applies even-handedly to all "substances that are illegal to minors."

Given the tragic consequences of teenage alcohol consumption—drinking causes far more fatal accidents than the misuse of marijuana—the school district's interest in deterring teenage alcohol use is at least comparable to its interest in preventing marijuana use. Under the Court's reasoning, must the First Amendment give way whenever a school seeks to punish a student for any speech mentioning beer, or indeed anything else that might be deemed risky to teenagers? While I find it hard to believe the Court would support punishing Frederick for flying a "WINE SiPS 4 JESUS" banner—which could quite reasonably be construed either as a protected religious message or as a pro-alcohol message—the breathtaking sweep of its opinion suggests it would.

Although this case began with a silly, nonsensical banner, it ends with the Court inventing out of whole cloth a special First Amendment rule permitting the censorship of any student speech that mentions drugs, at least so long as someone could perceive that speech to contain a latent pro-drug message. Our First Amendment jurisprudence has identified some categories of expression that are less deserving of protection than other—fighting words, obscenity, and commercial speech, to name a few. Rather than reviewing our opinions discussing such categories, I mention two personal recollections that have no doubt influenced my conclusion that it would be profoundly unwise to create special rules for speech about drug and alcohol use.

The Vietnam War is remembered today as an unpopular war. During its early stages, however, "the dominant opinion" that Justice Harlan mentioned in his *Tinker* dissent regarded opposition to the war as unpatriotic, if not treason.... In 1965, when the Des Moines students wore their armbands, the school district's fear that they might "start an argument or cause a disturbance" was well founded. *Tinker*. Given that context, there is special force to the Court's insistence that "our Constitution says we must take that risk; and our history says that it is this sort of hazardous freedom—this kind of openness—that is the basis of our national strength and of the independence and vigor of Americans who grow up and live in this relatively permissive, often disputatious, society." As we now know, the then-dominant opinion about the Vietnam War was not etched in stone.

Reaching back still further, the current dominant opinion supporting the war on drugs in general, and our anti-marijuana laws in particular, is reminiscent of the opinion that supported the nationwide ban on alcohol consumption when I was a student. While alcoholic beverages are now regarded as ordinary articles of commerce, their use was then condemned with the same moral fervor that now supports the war on drugs. . . .

Surely our national experience with alcohol should make us wary of dampening speech suggesting—however inarticulately—that it would be better to tax and regulate marijuana than to persevere in a futile effort to ban its use entirely.

Even in high school, a rule that permits only one point of view to be expressed is less likely to produce correct answers than the open discussion of countervailing views. In the national debate about a serious issue, it is the expression of the minority's viewpoint that most demands the protection of the First Amendment. Whatever the better policy may be, a full and frank discussion of the costs and benefits of the attempt to prohibit the use of marijuana is far wiser than suppression of speech because it is unpopular.

I respectfully dissent.

> *"There are few First Amendment violations clearer than a government employee's crumpling up someone's banner at a privately-sponsored rally on a public street."*

The School District Had an Exceptionally Weak Case

Julie Hilden

Julie Hilden is a Findlaw.com columnist and television legal commentator who formerly practiced law. The following column was written before the Supreme Court agreed to review Frederick v. Morse, *in which a high school student sued the school district because he was disciplined for displaying a banner the school principal found objectionable. (The names are reversed in the Supreme Court case because it was Morse, the principal, who appealed for the review.) In Hilden's opinion, the review should not have been sought because the violation of the student's First Amendment rights was clear and the Ninth Circuit Court ruled correctly. She says that the school's claim that to allow the banner would have been interpreted by the public as condoning illegal drug use was ridiculous, and that in ripping it up, the principal set a bad example of behavior that should not be defended.*

Last Monday, September 11 [2006], former Independent Counsel Kenneth Starr [known for his investigation of the scandal involving President Bill Clinton]—now a lawyer at Kirkland & Ellis—asked the Supreme Court to review a March

10 [2006] decision by the U.S. Court of Appeals for the Ninth Circuit, in the case of *Frederick v. Morse*. The decision upheld a public high school student's First Amendment right to display a banner off campus. Starr represents the school district on a pro bono [without charge] basis. . . .

The Facts of the *Frederick* Case

The *Frederick* case grew out of an incident in which Juneau, Alaska high school senior Joseph Frederick unfurled a banner reading "Bong Hits 4 Jesus" on a public sidewalk. He did so during a privately-sponsored rally where townspeople watched the Olympic torch pass by. Students were released from school to attend the rally. The high school's "pep band" and cheerleaders performed there, but the court found that teacher supervision of other students at the rally was "minimal or nonexistent."

Frederick and his friends made sure they unfurled their banner when TV cameras were passing by—but the school's principal, Deborah Morse, who was also attending the rally, went up to Frederick, grabbed the banner, crumpled it up, and suspended him for ten days.

Frederick later sued, invoking the federal civil rights statute that allows plaintiffs to seek money damages for government infringements of their constitutional rights, including First Amendment rights.

In my view, the principal's conduct was appalling. She didn't just tell Frederick to put his sign away, or that it was inappropriate, nor did she warn him that he could be suspended. Rather, she actually went right up to him on a public street and destroyed his banner.

This is the kind of thing that we believe cannot happen in this country. Is it suddenly acceptable simply because the victim is eighteen? What happened to school officials' duty to try to convince students—first, by setting the right example—to solve their differences with reason, not violence? Ironically, if

Frederick had ripped up another student's poster on school grounds, he surely would have been suspended for doing so.

In short, the example this principal is setting is a very ugly one. No wonder the Ninth Circuit held—on the separate question of the principal's claim to immunity under the federal civil rights statutes—that "it would be clear to a reasonable [principal] that [her] conduct was unlawful in the situation [she] confronted." (As a result, the principal herself may face liability for damages; she is a co-defendant in the case, along with the school board.)

How could this kind of behavior strike Starr, or Kirkland & Ellis, as so worthy of protecting, that it was worth taking this case on for the school district as a pro bono project?

The Legal Standards for Public School Students' Speech

There are three Supreme Court cases setting forth standards for public school students' speech—which were considered by the Ninth Circuit—but only one is relevant here.

One of the cases, *Hazelwood School Dist. v. Kuhlmeier*—addressing school-sponsored speech—doesn't apply because neither Frederick's banner (nor the rally itself) was school-sponsored in the sense that, for instance, a school-funded student newspaper is.

A second case, *Bethel School Dist. No. 3 v. Fraser*—which was relied on by the district court, but distinguished by the Ninth Circuit—doesn't apply because it addresses only vulgar, lewd, obscene, and otherwise "plainly offensive" speech, and because the Ninth Circuit has interpreted that to mean, in essence, obscenity or, at least, speech involving four-letter words or similarly profane language.

Finally, there is *Tinker v. Des Moines Independent Community School Dist.*. Its rule is simple: Student speech—other than speech that falls under the precedents noted above—can only be punished or otherwise regulated if it "materially disrupts classwork or involves substantial disorder or invasion of the rights of others." Moreover, to support the punishment or regulation, school districts must cite "evidence that [the punishment] is necessary to avoid material or substantial interference with schoolwork or discipline."

Applying the Legal Standard in the *Frederick* Case

The Juneau School District had an exceptionally weak case under *Tinker*.

In support of its case that Frederick's banner was disruptive, the District claimed that the banner would be read by many at the rally as "advocating or condoning illegal drug use."

Similarly, School Superintendent Peggy Cowan recently told CNN that this case is appropriate for Supreme Court review because it raises "an important question about how the First Amendment applies to pro-drug messages in an educational setting."

But even if this was, to some extent, a pro-drug message, that wasn't *all* it was. The district itself acknowledged that Frederick could have been not just responding to, but *parodying* the school's anti-drug message (and parody is strongly protected by the First Amendment). Moreover the "for Jesus" part shouldn't be left out of the analysis; juxtaposing "Bong Hits," the informal "4" for "for," and "Jesus" may also send a message that religion shouldn't be taken so seriously, and a message that Jesus was more laidback, and would have been more sympathetic to the counterculture, than some authoritarians would admit.

I'm not, of course, claiming that this message was well-thought out. To the contrary, it reads like a spur-of-the-moment lark, a prank. But I do think that it meant something different and more complicated, than just, say, a "Smoke Pot" banner would have. (Frederick himself said the banner was intended to be meaningless and funny, and he just wanted to get it on television. However, as many First Amendment cases have shown, words often have an impact beyond their intended meaning.)

The District also claimed that if the principal had done nothing, the district would have been seen by many as giving its imprimatur to Frederick's pro-drug message. But that claim seems ridiculous: If the District was as avid about spreading its anti-drug message as it claims that it was, no one would believe that it had suddenly changed its policy by merely deciding not to rip up Frederick's poster. If anything, onlookers might believe the District tolerated Frederick's poster out of a healthy respect for the First Amendment, or that the school district simply wasn't worried about its own message being undermined by a poorly-thought-out sophomoric sign.

Why the Ninth Circuit Is Right, and Starr Is Wrong, in This Case

Because this case is such a clear First Amendment violation, and because the Ninth Circuit rightly sided with the student, there's no good reason here for Supreme Court review.

In explaining why review was sought, Eric Hagen, an attorney from Starr's office who also worked on the Supreme Court petition, told a reporter, "It makes it a little harder when teachers and principals in their daily duties might be subject to a damages lawsuit and be held personally liable." But it's only harder for teachers and principals to perform their daily duties when the lines for liability are unclear.

As noted above, there are few First Amendment violations clearer than a government employee's crumpling up someone's banner at a privately-sponsored rally on a public street. That's censorship with a capital "C." If the Supreme Court does want to make the line between permissible disciplinary action and impermissible First Amendment violation clearer, perhaps it should wait for a subtler, closer case.

Ironically, I think most schoolchildren, if taught a bit about the First Amendment, could easily identify this as an obvious violation. Their teachers and principals ought at least to be able to do the same.

"Instead of asking whether school resources aided production *of speech, the Court should examine whether a student reached his chosen audience by participating in the school's expressive activity."*

Using School Events to Gain Publicity Is Different from Merely Exercising the Right to Free Speech

Murad Hussain

Murad Hussain is a third-year law student at Yale Law School. In the following viewpoint, written shortly before the Supreme Court heard Morse v. Frederick, *he argues that the Court could rule in favor of the school's effort to prevent undermining of its antidrug message without broadening restrictions on free speech. In this case, the student was not expressing ideas to other students with the aim of convincing them. Instead, he was using a school-sponsored event to attract TV cameras and get publicity for himself. In the earlier case* Hazelwood v. Kuhlmeier, *the Court established that if a school officially sponsors an activity it may censor the student speech involved. The Circuit Court considered this irrelevant because school resources were not used in the production of the banner to which the school objected. However, Hussain says, because a school rally was chosen for public dissemination of the student's message, the* Kuhlmeier *precedent could apply.*

Murad Hussain, "The 'Bong' Show: Viewing *Frederick's* Publicity Stunt through *Kuhlmeier's* Lens," *Yale Law Journal Pocket Part*, vol. 116, March 7, 2007, pp. 292-300. Copyright © 2007 The Yale Law Journal Company, Inc. Reprinted by permission of The Yale Law Journal Company, William S. Hein Company, and author.

In less than two weeks, the U.S. Supreme Court will hear argument in *Morse v. Frederick*. [The case was heard on March 19, 2007.] At issue is whether a public high school principal violated a student's First Amendment rights by suspending him for displaying a banner reading "BONG HiTS 4 JESUS" at an outdoor school rally for the 2002 Winter Olympics torch relay. The school petitioners, represented pro bono by Kenneth Starr, have urged the Court to give educators wide latitude to proscribe drug-themed speech so they can "foster and encourage a drug-free student lifestyle." Such broad authority would likely chill vital discourse within the school community. This Commentary suggests that the Court could endorse the power to punish students who turn school events into their personal public soapboxes without also letting schools suppress certain messages regardless of context. The Court could decide *Frederick* on narrower grounds, less threatening to expressive freedoms, by applying *Hazelwood School District v. Kuhlmeier*—the Court's only decision on censorship of student speech in school-sponsored activities that might reach audiences *outside* the school.

Background of the Case

Five years ago in Juneau, Alaska, then-senior Joseph Frederick hatched a plan to get on television. The Olympic torch, on its way to Salt Lake City, was going to pass in front of his high school during classes. The school board arranged for hundreds of students to watch from either side of the street under faculty supervision as the pep band played and cheerleaders stood ready to greet the four student torchbearers. Frederick and his friends picked a spot in the crowd easily visible to news crews filming the relay. As the runner and cameras approached, they unfurled their banner.

Principal Deborah Morse immediately suspended Frederick for violating the school's prohibition on displaying statements advocating drug use. Frederick sued her and the school board in federal district court, which ruled that *Bethel School District No. 403 v. Fraser* justified his punishment because his banner offended the school's "basic educational mission" of promoting healthy lifestyles. The Ninth Circuit reversed, holding that the banner was nondisruptive expression protected under *Tinker v. Des Moines Independent Community School District* and that Frederick's rights were so clearly established that Principal Morse did not merit qualified immunity. [Immunity from being sued personally for money.]

The grant of certiorari [review] likely surprised those who saw *Frederick* as a simple case of political expression that merely required rote application of *Tinker*. But in fact, the Court re-listed *Frederick* four times before deciding to hear it, possibly because the Justices were considering summary reversal of the qualified immunity ruling before ultimately voting to review the merits question as well. Legal observers now expect the Court to "clarify" the relationship between *Tinker*, which protected three students' right to wear antiwar armbands to school, and *Fraser*, which upheld a student's suspension for delivering a "plainly offensive" sexually suggestive speech at a student government assembly.

Tinker, decided in 1969 and authored by Justice Fortas, provided an outlet for peaceful student dissent by holding that schools may only restrict "personal intercommunication among the students" if such discourse threatens to disrupt the school's work or to invade others' rights. *Fraser* later limited *Tinker's* scope by broadly construing the "basic educational mission" to include promoting civil discourse by "teaching students the boundaries of socially appropriate behavior." Resurrecting Justice Black's vigorous *Tinker* dissent, *Fraser* deferred to a school's conclusion that "vulgar speech and lewd conduct [are] wholly inconsistent with the 'fundamental values' of public school education."

School Claimed Banner Undercut Antidrug Message

The petitioners in *Frederick*, Principal Morse and the Juneau School Board, argue that the "special characteristics" of public schools necessarily constrain students' constitutional rights. They ask the Court to expand *Fraser's* concept of the "educational mission" to include the Juneau school district's promotion of a drug-free lifestyle. The petitioners also justify Frederick's punishment on the theory that his banner undercut their efforts to comply with their federally funded mandate to deliver a consistent anti-drug message. This argument may resonate with those on the Court—including Justices Breyer and Kennedy—who joined two recent Fourth Amendment opinions upholding suspicionless drug testing policies for students participating in extracurricular activities. Those decisions similarly declared that "'special needs' inhere in the public school context" because educators have a unique "custodial and tutelary responsibility for children." In the more recent of the two cases, Justice Breyer also concurred separately to emphasize the "serious national problem" of student drug abuse. Citing *Fraser's* proposition that schools must prepare youth for citizenship, he suggested that the policy of random urinalysis fell squarely within the school's *in loco parentis* duty to protect students by minimizing the appeal of drug culture. Given that Justice Breyer has long been considered a First Amendment pragmatist, his emphatic anti-drug orientation suggests he may be a pivotal voice in the Court's disposition of *Frederick*.

However, letting schools restrict expression that conflicts with specific governmental policies could swallow *Tinker's* protections for intra-school dissent. Under the guise of enforcing protective agendas, administrators might feel free to punish students whose speech counters their own political inclinations. As if to prove the point, the *Frederick* petitioners have implied that anti-drug policies should validate censorship of political messages like the T-shirt criticizing President Bush as a former addict that was the subject of a recent Second Circuit decision. Permitting broader content regulation would likely embolden schools' promulgation and defense of speech codes, chilling expression on both sides of the ideological divide. The Sixth Circuit has already upheld a school's ban on Marilyn Manson T-shirts, which the principal justified partly on one image's anti-religious content, while another recent Ninth Circuit decision upheld a student's suspension for wearing a shirt bearing a religiously motivated anti-gay message. If *Frederick* turns *Fraser's* solicitude for civility norms into a general license to punish certain ideas, that could leave students too afraid to exercise the "hazardous freedom" of open discourse that is so essential to their education.

Public Expression Is Different from Speech to Students

The Court can avoid this treacherous path while still letting schools discipline students in Frederick's specific situation under a different theory altogether—a theory derived from *Hazelwood School District v. Kuhlmeier*. In *Kuhlmeier*, decided two years after *Fraser*, the Court rejected three students' challenge to their principal's censorship of the school newspaper. The Court found that *Tinker's* nondisruption test was inappropriate for the narrower context of a school-sponsored "expressive activit[y]" that "students, *parents, and members of the public*" might perceive as bearing the school's "imprimatur." Instead, the Court held that a school's refusal "to lend its name and resources to the dissemination of student expression"—such as speech advocating drug use—need simply be "reasonably related to legitimate pedagogical concerns."

The Court could interpret Frederick's banner as speech in a *publicly* directed expressive activity of the kind that only *Kuhlmeier* has contemplated. Unlike the purely intra-school discourse in *Tinker* or *Fraser*, expressive activities such as plays and concerts are forums in which student speech is often managed for dissemination beyond the school. When schools sponsor such activities for the education and enjoyment of student participants and public audiences alike, the schools function not just as inwardly focused educational instruments but also as civic institutions engaging the citizens who support them. The *Frederick* petitioners had concluded that the torch relay's educational and community value warranted giving students an opportunity to publicly celebrate their pride in their torch-bearing classmates. Like plays and concerts, the rally could be viewed as an opportunity for the school, through its students, to express its commitment to the wider community. This civic mission is distinct from the educational mission of fostering deliberation solely within the school to encourage free-thinking or to instill social values. *Kuhlmeier's* unique concern for the perception of a school's imprimatur by those outside the school community hinted at the value of this separate institutional persona.

Kuhlmeier also distinguished its analysis of "school-sponsored ... vehicle[s] of student expression" from *Tinker* and *Fraser's* discussions of speech "that happens to occur" at school. Frederick's reason for picking the school's rally as his venue—namely, his desire to be on television—shows that his speech did not merely "happen[] to occur" at the rally, and that it was not intended to be part of the "personal intercommunication among students" that the *Tinker* Court sought to protect. While *Tinker* praised the students for silently wearing their armbands in school "to make their views known, and, by their example, to influence others to adopt them," Frederick was not trying to sway his classmates' opinions about anything, whether marijuana, the Messiah, or the latter's preference for the former. Rather, he only wanted "to attract television cameras." Although he could have stood anywhere along the main avenue's half-mile stretch, the school's rally was the most thematically logical backdrop for the news spotlight on the student torchbearers. Frederick specifically chose to express himself at the rally so that he could appropriate its publicity and steal the spotlight for himself.

School Resources Were Used to Disseminate Ideas

When the Ninth Circuit concluded that *Kuhlmeier* was inapplicable, it focused too narrowly on the example of a school newspaper and whether Frederick used school resources to produce his banner. This analysis ignored *Kuhlmeier's* express concern for the use of school resources to *disseminate* speech. In live school-sponsored venues, bold students can deviate from messages they have been given the opportunity to express, and yet the school will have disseminated their speech despite contributing no physical resources to the act of expression. A production-oriented sponsorship analysis would thus have left Principal Morse helpless if the pep band, using personally owned instruments, had decided to play Bob Dylan's "Rainy Day Women #12 & 35" while leading the crowd in a singalong of "*Everybody must get stoned....*"

Instead of asking whether school resources aided *production of speech*, the Court should examine whether a student reached his chosen audience by participating in the school's expressive activity. Under such an inquiry, a live event's publicity and audience become dissemination-promoting resources. In *Frederick*, the school's imprimatur on the rally enabled students to gather outside during class for a civic celebratory purpose. By giving students' sentiments a public airing, the school generated publicity by creating a media-friendly backdrop for the torch relay. Without the school's permission, students would not have been allowed outside, and Frederick may not have received his desired television audience even if he had cut class in order to stand all alone in front of the school. The rally could therefore be seen as facilitating the public dissemination of Frederick's message to the passing cameras.

By viewing Frederick's publicity stunt through *Kuhlmeier's* lens, the Court could endorse the school's decision to discipline Frederick while narrowly defining the context in which educators may regulate drug-themed speech. Although this would be a defeat for Frederick individually, such a ruling would not be the setback for First Amendment protections that an expansion of *Fraser* might. At the very least, it would be unfortunate if the Court broadly reshapes the contours of intra-school discourse with an idiosyncratic case in which the student was not trying to speak to anyone at school.

> "There [was] an effort to prevent a message that is inconsistent with a fundamental message of the schools and we believe that is permitted under Tinker."

School Officials Have a Right to Suppress Speech Advocating Illegal Actions

Kenneth Starr and Justices of the Supreme Court

Kenneth Starr is a lawyer and former judge; he is best known as the U. S. independent counsel who produced the Starr Report about the scandal involving President Bill Clinton and Monica Lewinsky. The following selection is his oral argument before the Supreme Court in Morse v. Frederick. *He is representing Deborah Morse, a school principal who appealed to the Supreme Court for review after losing her case in the Circuit Court. That court ruled that she was wrong to tear down the banner displayed by student Joseph Frederick because he had a constitutional right to free speech even though, in her opinion, his message undermined the school's mission to discourage use of illegal drugs. During the argument, Starr was questioned by the Supreme Court justices. The transcript reveals some of the kinds of issues they consider before deciding a case.*

M*r. Starr:* Chief Justice, and may it please the Court:

Illegal drugs and the glorification of the drug culture are profoundly serious problems for our nation. Congress has so

Kenneth Star, and Justices of the Supreme Court, oral argument in *Deborah Morse et al. v. Joseph Frederick*, U.S. Supreme Court, March 19, 2007.

recognized, as has this Court, time and again. The magnitude of the problem is captured in the amicus [friend of the court] brief, the Court has a number of amicus briefs before it, but the amicus brief of General [Barry] McCaffrey, Secretary [William] Bennett, and a number of organizations. And particularly, pages 5 to 9 of that brief, the nature and the scope of the problem are well-captured.

Justice [Anthony] Kennedy: Well, is this case limited to signs about drugs? What is the rule that you want us to adopt for deciding this case?

Mr. Starr: The rule the Court—that it articulated in *Tinker*. The rule of the Court as articulated in *Tinker* is that there is, in fact, a right to political speech subject to disruption, requirements that the speech not be disruptive.

Justice Kennedy: Disruptive of what? Disruptive of the classroom order? There was no classroom here.

Mr. Starr: Including but not limited to. This was a school authorized event, this was education outside of the classroom. It was essentially a school simply out of doors.

Justice [David] Souter: Well, I can understand if they unfurled the banner in a classroom that it would be disruptive, but what did it disrupt on the sidewalk?

Mr. Starr: The educational mission of the school.

What Makes Student Speech Disruptive?

Justice Souter: No, but I mean, that's at a level of generality that doesn't get us very far. I mean, what specifically did it disrupt? Did it disrupt the parade, did it disrupt teaching, what was it?

Mr. Starr: 5520, a school policy of the board that says emphatically that political speech is protected, embracing *Tinker*.

Justice Souter: Then if that's the rule, the school can make any rule that it wants on any subject restrictive of speech, and if anyone violates it, the result is, on your reasoning, it's disruptive under *Tinker*.

Mr. Starr: Not at all. . . .

Justice Souter: Then I'm missing the argument.

Mr. Starr: The argument is that this Court in *Tinker* articulated a rule that allows the school boards considerable discretion both in identifying the educational mission and to prevent disruption of that mission, and this is disruptive of the mission—

Justice Kennedy: Well, suppose you have—suppose you have a mission to have a global school. Can they ban American flags on lapel pins?

Mr. Starr: Absolutely not, because under *Tinker* that is political expression. Let me be very specific. This case is ultimately about drugs and other illegal substances.

Justice [Ruth Bader] Ginsburg: So if the sign had been "Bong Stinks for Jesus," that would be, and Morse had the same reaction, that this was demeaning to the Olympics and it was unruly conduct, that there would be a protected right under *Tinker* because the message was not promoting drugs?

Was the Sign Political?

Mr. Starr: She stated in her answers to interrogatories [pretrial questioning] that she may very well not have interfered with the banner had it in fact said legalize marijuana. Under our theory, we think she could have interfered with that because it was disruptive to the event, it was disorderly to the event itself, but the—

Justice Souter: What would be disorderly? I don't understand this disorder. If somebody holds up a sign and says change the marijuana laws, why is it disruptive of anything, simply because the school quite naturally has said we support the enforcement of the law, and the law right now does forbid the use of marijuana. . . .

It's political speech, it seems to me. I don't see what it disrupts, unless disruption simply means any statement of disagreement with a position officially adopted by the school. Is that what you mean by disruption?

Mr. Starr: No. Your Honor, first of all, this is, I think, an unusual characterization, namely for this to be called political speech. . . .

Justice Souter: A call for a change in the law, I would have supposed, was political speech.

Mr. Starr: That wasn't the interpretation. Your Honor, let's back up, if I may. Someone has to interpret the message and the front line message interpreter is the school official.

Justice Souter: Well, that may be, but that's not the hypo. The hypothetical is, what if there is a sign or a statement in the school calling for a change in, you know, the prohibition against marijuana use? As a call for change in the law, I would suppose it was political speech. But as I understood the argument you were making, it would still be regarded as an exception, as it were, to *Tinker*, because it was disruptive. And it was disruptive in the sense that it disagreed with official school policy, which was to enforce the law or support the law as it was. Is that your position on what disruption means under *Tinker*?

Tinker Is Not the Only Precedent

Mr. Starr: But our—the answer is no. Because what we are also urging the Court to consider is its gloss on *Tinker* and *Fra[s]er*, and also what this Court said in *Kuhlmeier*. And in *Fra[s]er*, the Court was very clear, . . . in talking about the habits and manners of civility, and inculcating the values of citizenship. That, in fact, is what is happening here. There is an effort to prevent a message that is inconsistent with a fundamental message of the schools, which is the use of illegal drugs is simply verboten, and we believe that is permitted under *Tinker*—. . .

Justice [Antonin] Scalia: This banner was interpreted as meaning smoke pot, no?

Mr. Starr: It was interpreted—exactly, yes. It was interpreted as an encouragement of the drug culture and—

Justice [Samuel] Alito: Are you arguing that there should be a sui generis [unique] rule for speech that advocates illegal drug use, or this broader argument that the school can suppress any speech that is inconsistent with its educational mission as the school . . . defines it?

Mr. Starr: The Court can certainly decide this on very narrow grounds, that there are certain substances, illegal drugs, we would include alcohol and tobacco, that's part of the school's policy, because those are illegal substances which are very injurious to health. And this Court has noted that in [V]ernonia and in Earls, time and again, it is that these are very dangerous substances and we have a clear policy sanctioned by Congress, and also noted by courts across the country, that illegal drugs are so dangerous that schools are entitled to have a message going—

Chief Justice [John] Roberts: But the problem—the problem, Mr. Starr, is that school boards these days take it upon themselves to broaden their mission well beyond education or protection from illegal substances, and several of the briefs have pointed out school boards have adopted policies taking on the whole range of political issues. Now, do they get to dictate the content of speech on all of those issues simply because they have adopted that as the part of their educational mission?

Mr. Starr: No, because that may very well be inconsistent with Tinker. Tinker articulates a baseline of political speech is, in fact, protected, subject to—

How Broadly Should Tinker Be Interpreted?

Chief Justice Roberts: Well, I think that you're right about that, and I guess my question goes to how broadly we should read Tinker. I mean, why is it that the classroom ought to be a forum for political debate simply because the students want to put that on their agenda? Presumably the teacher's agenda is a little bit different and includes things like teaching Shakespeare or the Pythagorean Theorem, and just because political speech is on the student's agenda, I'm not sure that it makes sense to read *Tinker* so broadly as to include protection of those, that speech.

Mr. Starr: This Court has not read *Tinker* quite so broadly in both *Fra[s]er* and in *Kuhlmeier*, and there are a couple of aspects of *Tinker* that I think are worthy of note. One, that there was no written policy there, so there was an issue of standardless discretion being exercised. And also—

Justice Ginsburg: But it may have made a difference in *Tinker*. If the school had a policy, defend our troops in Vietnam, would that have brought this into the category that you are now carving out? You said that *Tinker* had no policy, but suppose the school did have a policy, patriotism, we support our troops, no bad speech about the war in Vietnam. Should *Tinker* have come out the other way?

Mr. Starr: No, it should not, because there—I think there are concerns with respect to what this Court has identified it is trying to, even in the public school setting, quite apart from the university setting, to cast a pall of orthodoxy to prevent the discussion of ideas. What is happening here of course in this case, it can be decided very narrowly, that drugs, alcohol and tobacco just have no place in the schools. And—

Justice Kennedy: Yes, but the rule you proposed, I thought, in response to my question is that the school has wide discretion to define its educational mission and it can restrict speech that's inconsistent with that mission. . . .

Mr. Starr: Justice Kennedy, the words that you articulated are essentially quotes of *Fra[s]er* and *Kuhlmeier*, so there is a broadening of the lens and a restoration, frankly, of greater school discretion in those two cases than one might see in *Tinker*. They of course drew, as you well know, from Justice Black's warning in dissent of *Tinker* that the Federal courts,

Federal judiciary should not be extending itself unduly into the work of the school boards'—

Surely Schools Can Discourage Lawbreaking

Justice Scalia: Why do we have to get into the question of what the school board's policy is and what things they can make its policy? Surely it can be the—it must be the policy of any school to discourage breaking of the law. I mean, suppose this banner had said kill somebody, and there was no explicit regulation of the school that said you should not, you should not foster murder. Wouldn't that be suppressible?. . .

Why can't we decide this case on that narrow enough ground, that any school whether it has expressed the policy or not, can suppress speech that advocates violation of the law?

Mr. Starr: I think it can, but it raises some interesting potential hypothetical questions, what about listening to the voice of Martin Luther King Junior, conscientious objection and so forth. I don't think the Court needs to stray into those areas because here we have a written policy which does in fact respond to concerns about the exercise of standardless discretion.

Justice [John] Stevens: Let me just clear up one thing to be 100 percent sure I understand your position. It does—the message is the critical part of this case. If it was a totally neutral message on a 15-foot sign, that would be okay. You're not saying 15-foot signs are disruptive?

Mr. Starr: Not inherently disruptive, but in fact—the answer is yes. We're not saying that.

Justice Stevens: And so we're focusing on the message and that's the whole crux of the case.

Mr. Starr: That's why this case is here because of the message.

Justice [Stephen] Breyer: Well, why is that? Why? Why? I mean suppose you go on a school trip, and the teacher says on the school trip, I don't want people unfurling 15 foot banners. I don't care what they are about. . . .

Mr. Starr: In response to Justice Stevens' question, the message here is in fact critical. . .

The Parade Was a School Event

Justice Stevens: It's also critical here to your case that it was a school event. If it, if this had have been two blocks down the street there would have been no objection.

Mr. Starr: If Mr. Frederick had seen fit to go down Glacier Avenue to J and J's, a popular hangout, there would have been no high school jurisdiction. There may have been elementary school—but yes. He could have gone, Justice Stevens, to the State capital or anywhere along the ten mile route. . . .

Justice Ginsburg: Suppose it were Saturday, not a school day. And the school children were not required to show up at the Olympic event but were encouraged to and the same thing happened. Would it make a difference that it wasn't in the course of a regular school day?

Mr. Starr: No. I think it still, under your hypothetical would be school sponsored. But there might be a more difficult showing of disruption or inconsistency with the educational mission. That is what this Court articulated in *Fra[s]er* and again in *Kuhlmeier* that the school is able under our policies of federalism and value of federalism and democratic theory to fashion its educational mission subject to constitutional safeguards. And that mission of preventing the schools from being infected with pro-drug messages continues wherever there is school jurisdiction, and that would include on a Saturday field trip or other kind of activity and I think that—

Justice Scalia: Mr. Starr, you—you responded to Justice Breyer that you think the school could just prohibit the unfurling of 15 foot banners on a trip. Could it prohibit the wearing of black armbands on a trip?

Mr. Starr: I don't believe so.

Justice Scalia: And if not—if not, what's the difference?

Mr. Starr: Because of the potential for disruption, disorderliness in the event and the judgment that is entrusted to—

Different Kinds of Disruption

Justice Souter: But don't we have to be more specific about the context in determining whether there's disruption? If it's a school trip to an art museum, unfurling a 15 foot banner in front of the pictures is clearly going to be disruptive of the object of the trip. Unfurling a banner in a classroom is going to be disruptive to the teaching of Shakespeare or whatever is supposed to be going on in there.

What we have here is the unfurling of a banner on a sidewalk in a crowd with kids throwing snowballs waiting for somebody to run by with a TV camera nearby. And there is a real question as to whether, it seems to me, as to whether it is in a kind of practical, real world sense, disruptive of anything. And if there is such a question, shouldn't the answer favor the right to, to make the speech as opposed to favor the right to suppress it?

Mr. Starr: Your Honor, the answer is no.

We do think that if the test that this Court has articulated which we embrace, looks not simply to "disruption" but inconsistency with what this Court has focused—this Court's language, the basic educational mission, then surely—

Justice Souter: All right. Let me, let me follow, actually ask you the same question on that. Because in response to Justice Scalia's question you said certainly that the school has got the right to have a policy that forbids violating the law and calling for violations of the law.

Accepting that as a premise, don't we need, before the school may suppress the speech, don't we need at least a statement which is clearly inconsistent with that policy? And if that is so, is Bong Hits 4 Jesus inconsistent with it? It sounds like just a kid's provocative statement to me.

The School Official Should Be Allowed to Interpret the Message

Mr. Starr: Your Honor, with all due respect, the key is to allow the school official to interpret the message as long as that interpretation is reasonable. You might disagree with that just as Justice Brennan disagreed with whether Matt Frazer's speech was all that terrible. But he said even though it wasn't all that terrible I nonetheless defer to the interpretation of school officials. That's what our educational system is about.

Justice Ginsburg: But those were the words and characterizing them as offensive, but here one could look at these words and say it's just nonsense. Or one could say it's like mares-eat-oats. It isn't clear that this is "smoke pot."

Mr. Starr: Your Honor, again, Deborah Morse, a conscientious principal, interpreted the message in light of the subculture of the school where drug use is a serious problem. And it was on the spot judgment. We believe that judgment was reasonable as opposed to a judgment reached in judicial chambers, but we know that that was also the judgment of the superintendent and district judge—

Justice Stevens: Is that a judgment clear enough as a matter of law, or is there possible debate as to whether that's a reasonable interpretation of the message? Let's assume it was an ambiguous message. Would we have to accept her interpretation on summary judgment?

Mr. Starr: Yes, I believe you do. And—well, that's of course a question for the district judge. And here the judge analyzed the facts in terms of what the individual was trying to say and determined that that is a reasonable interpretation and that is all that is required under this Court's law.

I'd like to reserve the remainder of my time. Thank you.

Chief Justice Roberts: Thank you, Counsel.

Organizations to Contact

The editors have compiled the following list of organizations concerned with the issues debated in this book. The descriptions are derived from materials provided by the organizations. All have publications or information available for interested readers. The list was compiled on the date of publication of the present volume; the information provided here may change. Be aware that many organizations take several weeks or longer to respond to inquiries, so allow as much time as possible.

American Civil Liberties Union (ACLU)

125 Broad Street, 18th Floor, New York, NY   10004
Web site: www aclu.org

The ACLU is a large national organization that works to preserve First Amendment rights—freedom of speech, freedom of association and assembly, freedom of the press, and freedom of religion supported by the strict separation of church and state—as well as the right to equal protection under the law regardless of race, sex, religion or national origin; the right to due process; and the right to freedom from unwarranted government intrusion into personal and private affairs. It provides legal assistance in cases that involve these rights. Its Web site offers many articles and it can be contacted for more information through online forms.

American Library Association (ALA)

50 East Huron Street, Chicago, IL   60611
(800) 545-2433
e-mail: oif@ala.org
Web site: www.ala.org/oif

The ALA is the national professional association for librarians. It strongly supports freedom of speech, and through its Office for Intellectual Freedom (OIF) Web site it offers a large amount of material on related issues, including news, commentary, and basic information for both adults and young people.

First Amendment Center
1207 18th Ave. S., Nashville, TN 37212
(615) 727-1600 • fax: (615) 727-1319
e-mail: info@fac.org
Web site: www.firstamendmentcenter.org

The First Amendment Center, which is affiliated with Vanderbilt University, works to preserve and protect First Amendment freedoms through information and education. The center serves as a forum for the study and exploration of free-expression issues, including freedom of speech, of the press and of religion, and the rights to assemble and to petition the government. Its Web site offers many articles and report, including a PDF version of the book *The Silencing of Student Voices: The Challenge to Free Speech in America's Schools.*

First Amendment Project (FAP)
736 Franklin St., 9th Floor, Oakland, CA 94612
(510) 208-7744 • Fax: (510) 208-4562
e-mail: fap@thefirstamendment.org
www.thefirstamendment.org

FAP is a nonprofit advocacy organization dedicated to protecting and promoting freedom of information, expression, and petition. It provides advice, educational materials, and legal representation to its core constituency of activists, journalists, and artists. Its Web site offers guides and handbooks focused on legal issues, activism, and the process of gaining access to information.

Free Speech Coalition
PO Box 10480, Canoga Park, CA 91309
(818) 348-9373
Web site: www.freespeechcoalition.com

The Free Speech Coalition is a trade association for the adult entertainment industry. Its mission is to lead, protect, and support the growth and well-being of the adult entertainment community, which it often does through litigation. Its Web site contains detailed information about court cases such as *Ashcroft v. Free Speech Coalition* (see Chapter 3 of this book).

National Coalition Against Censorship (NCAC)
275 Seventh Avenue, #1504, New York, NY   10001
(212) 807-6222 • fax: (212) 807-6245
e-mail: ncac@ncac.org
Web site: www.ncac.org

The NCAC is an alliance of fifty national nonprofit organizations, including literary, artistic, religious, educational, professional, labor, and civil liberties groups. United by a conviction that freedom of thought, inquiry, and expression must be defended, it works to educate members and the public at large about the dangers of censorship and how to oppose them. Its Web site contains commentary on news about free speech and related issues, back issues of its quarterly newsletter *Censorship News*, and information on books that can be ordered.

People for the American Way
2000 M Street NW, Suite 400, Washington, DC   20036
(202) 467-4999
e-mail: pfaw@pfaw.org
Web site: www.pfaw.org

People for the American Way is a nonprofit educational organization that is engaged in lobbying and other forms of political activism. Its purpose is to affirm "the American Way," by which it means pluralism; individuality; freedom of thought, expression, and religion; a sense of community; and tolerance and compassion for others. Its Web site contains press releases about recent and upcoming court cases involving constitutional liberties.

Student Press Law Center (SPLC)
1101 Wilson Blvd., Suite 1100, Arlington, VA 22209
(703) 807-1904
Web site: www.splc.org

The Student Press Law Center is a nonprofit, nonpartisan legal assistance agency devoted exclusively to educating high school and college journalists about the rights and responsibilities embodied in the First Amendment and supporting the student news media in their struggle to cover important issues free from censorship. The center provides free legal advice and information as well as low-cost educational materials for student journalists. It publishes a quarterly magazine, the *SPLC Report*, and back issues are available for reading at its Web site as well as other publications that can be ordered.

Supreme Court of the United States
Public Information Officer, Supreme Court of the United States
Washington, DC 20543
Web site: www.supremecourtus.gov

The Supreme Court's official Web site contains detailed descriptions of the Court and how it operates. It also has briefs, transcripts of oral arguments, and opinions in recent cases, as well as information about scheduled cases.

For Further Research

Books

Henry Julian Abraham and Barbara A. Perry, *Freedom and the Court: Civil Rights and Liberties in the United States.* Lawrence: University Press of Kansas, 2003.

Floyd Abrams, *Speaking Freely: Trials of the First Amendment.* New York: Penguin, 2006.

George Anastaplo, *Reflections on Freedom of Speech and the First Amendment.* Lexington: University Press of Kentucky, 2006.

Richard Arum, *Judging School Discipline: The Crisis of Moral Authority.* Cambridge, MA: Harvard University Press, 2003.

Lee C. Bollinger and Geoffrey R. Stone, eds., *Eternally Vigilant: Free Speech in the Modern Era.* Chicago: University of Chicago Press, 2002.

Stephen Breyer, *Active Liberty: Interpreting Our Democratic Constitution.* New York: Knopf, 2005.

Raphael Cohen-Almagor, *Speech, Media and Ethics: The Limits of Free Expression.* New York: Palgrave Macmillan, 2005.

Michael C. Dorf, ed., *Constitutional Law Stories.* New York: Foundation Press, 2004.

Christopher M. Finan, *From the Palmer Raids to the Patriot Act: A History of the Fight for Free Speech in America.* Boston: Beacon, 2007.

Mike Godwin, *Cyber Rights: Defending Free Speech in the Digital Age.* Cambridge, MA: MIT Press, 2003.

John B. Gould, *Speak No Evil: The Triumph of Hate Speech Regulation.* Chicago: University of Chicago Press, 2005.

Marjorie Heins, *Not in Front of the Children: "Indecency," Censorship, and the Innocence of Youth.* New Brunswick, NJ: Rutgers University Press, 2008.

David L. Hudson Jr., The *Silencing of Student Voices: The Challenge to Free Speech in America's Schools.* Nashville, TN: First Amendment Center, 2003.

Peter H. Irons, *The Courage of Their Convictions: Sixteen Americans Who Fought Their Way to the Supreme Court.* New York: Penguin, 1990. (Includes Mary Beth Tinker.)

Peter H. Irons, *May It Please the Court: Courts, Kids, and the Constitution: Live Recordings and Transcripts of Sixteen Supreme Court Oral Arguments on the Constitutional Rights of Students and Teachers.* New York: New Press, 2000. (Includes *Tinker v. Des Moines* and *Hazelwood v. Kuhlmeier.*)

Thomas A. Jacobs, *Teens Take It to Court: Young People Who Challenged the Law—and Changed Your Life.* Minneapolis: Free Spirit, 2006. (Includes *Tinker v. Des Moines* and *Hazelwood v. Kuhlmeier.*)

John W. Johnson, *The Struggle for Student Rights:* Tinker v. Des Moines *and the 1960s.* Lawrence: University Press of Kansas, 1997.

Nan Levinson, *Outspoken: Free Speech Stories.* Berkeley: University of California Press, 2003.

David Lowenthal, *Present Dangers: Rediscovering the First Amendment.* Dallas, TX: Spence, 2003.

Samuel P. Nelson, *Beyond the First Amendment: The Politics of Free Speech and Pluralism.* Baltimore: Johns Hopkins University Press, 2005.

Laura Beth Nielsen, *License to Harass: Law, Hierarchy, and Offensive Public Speech*. Princeton, NJ: Princeton University Press, 2006.

Richard A. Parker, ed., *Free Speech on Trial: Communication Perspectives on Landmark Supreme Court Decisions*. Tuscaloosa: University of Alabama Press, 2003.

John Durham Peters, *Courting the Abyss: Free Speech and the Liberal Tradition*. Chicago: University of Chicago Press, 2005.

Jamin B. Raskin, *We the Students: Supreme Court Decisions For and About Students*. Washington, DC: CQ, 2003.

Joseph Russomanno, *Speaking Our Minds: Conversations with the People behind Landmark First Amendment Cases*. Mahwah, NJ: Lawrence Erlbaum Associates, 2002.

Joseph Russomanno, ed., *Defending the First: Commentary on the First Amendment Issues and Cases*. Mahwah, NJ: Lawrence Erlbaum Associates, 2005.

Kevin Saunders, *Saving Our Children from the First Amendment*. New York: New York University Press, 2006.

Harvey A. Silverglate, David A. French, and Greg Lukianoff, *FIRE's Guide to Free Speech on Campus*. Philadelphia: Foundation for Individual Rights in Education, 2004.

Laura Stein, *Speech Rights in America: The First Amendment, Democracy, and the Media*. Urbana: University of Illinois Press, 2006.

Geoffrey R. Stone, *Perilous Times: Free Speech in Wartime: From the Sedition Act of 1798 to the War on Terrorism*. New York: W.W. Norton, 2004.

Thomas L. Tedford and Dale A. Herbeck, *Freedom of Speech in the United States*, 5th ed. State College, PA: Strata, 2005.

Periodicals

Robert Barnes, "Justices to Hear Landmark Free-Speech Case," *Washington Post*, March 13, 2007.

Daniel W. Bower, "Holding Virtual Child Pornography Creators Liable by Judicial Redress: An Alternative Approach to Overcoming the Obstacles Presented in *Ashcroft v. Free Speech Coalition*," *BYU Journal of Public Law*, Fall 2004.

Daniel Burke, "Supreme Court Hears 'Bong Hits 4 Jesus' Case," *ChristianityToday.com*, March (Web only) 2007.

Debra D. Burke, "Thinking Outside the Box: Child Pornography, Obscenity and the Constitution," *Virginia Journal of Law and Technology*, Fall 2003.

Glenn Cook, "A Sign of the Times," *American School Board Journal*, May 2007.

Christa S. Cothrel, "The Continuing Criminality of Virtual Child Pornography in the Wake of the *Ashcroft* Decision," *Reporter*, June 2002.

Mark Goodman, "Student Journalism after *Hazelwood*," *American Editor*, July/August 1996.

Linda Greenhouse, "Free-Speech Case Divides Bush and Religious Right," *New York Times*, March 18, 2007.

Terrence P. Jeffrey, "Bush Demands Zero Tolerance for Kiddie Porn," *Human Events*, November 4, 2002.

Daniel Henninger, "Bong Hits 4 Jesus—Final Episode," *Wall Street Journal*, June 28, 2007.

Susan S. Kreston, "Defeating the Virtual Defense in Child Pornography Decisions," *Journal of High Technology Law*, 2004.

Charles Lane, "Court Backs School on Speech Curbs," *Washington Post*, June 26, 2007.

Louis P. Nappen, "School Safety v. Free Speech," *Texas Journal on Civil Liberties & Civil Rights*, 2003.

Don Oldenburg, "Wearing the Right to Free Speech on Her Sleeve," *Washington Post*, September 16, 2005.

Elizabeth A. Palmer, "Foes of 'Virtual' Child Pornography Seeking a Very Real Remedy After Court Strikes Down Ban," *CQ Weekly*, April 20, 2002.

Jamin B. Raskin & Mary Beth Tinker, "Black Armbands for Constitution Day," *Education Week*, September 7, 2005.

Joseph Russomanno, "Dissent Yesterday and Today: The *Tinker* Case and Its Legacy," *Communication Law & Policy*, Summer 2006.

Taylor Smith, "Lost in Translation—Adapting to Child Pornography Prosecutions After *Ashcroft v. Free Speech Coalition*," *Reporter*, June 2004.

Alan J. Sofalvi, "The *Hazelwood* Decision and the Health Education Curriculum," *Journal of School Health*, September 2000.

Claudia Mansfield Sutton, "Court Backs Administrators' Right to Protect Students' Best Interests," *USA Today*, June 26, 2007.

Andrew Trotter, "Justices Differ Sharply on Student Speech," *Education Week*, March 28, 2007.

Mark Walsh, "Rights at Stake in Free-Speech Case," *Education Week*, March 9, 2007.

Steven Winn, "High Court or Theater of the Absurd?" *San Francisco Chronicle*, March 28, 2007.

Pete Yost, "Court Limits Student Free-Speech Rights," *Los Angeles Times*, June 25, 2007.

Perry A. Zirkel, "The 30th Anniversary of *Tinker*," *Phi Delta Kappan*, September 1999.

Index

A

Adult *vs.* student rights, 58–59, 145, 149, 154

Adversarial legalism, 39–40

Advocacy issues, 159–160

Affirmative defense, 113–114

Alito, Samuel, 181

Alternative newspapers, 88–89

American Beauty (film), 108, 117, 119–120

American Civil Liberties Union, 82

Anacostia neighborhood, 38–39

Anonymity issues, 64

Arizona, Miranda v. See Miranda v. Arizona

Armbands, 19–20, 22–26, 46–48, 92, 155, 184

Art, 126

Arum, Richard, 39

Ashcroft v. Free Speech Coalition (2002)

    all speech should be free, 131–139

    case overview, 101–102

    child abuse, effect on, 123–126

    dissenting opinion, 116–122

    majority opinion, 103–115

    pornography as exception to First Amendment rights, 127–130

B

Bad speech, 132–134

Barnette, West Virginia Board of Education v. See West Virginia Board of Education v. Barnette

Bartels v. Iowa, 23

Baxter v. Vigo County, 97

Bethel School District v. Fraser (1986)

    applicability to *Deborah Morse et al. v. Joseph Frederick,* 165, 171

    applicability to *Hazelwood School District v. Kuhlmeier,* 59, 63, 68, 69, 85

    indecent speech, 145, 148

    offensive speech, 151

    students' First Amendment rights, 93

Black, Hugo, 30–37, 43, 171, 182–183

Black, Virginia v. See Virginia v. Black

Black armbands. *See* Armbands

Blackmun, Harry, 66, 87

Board of Education, Brown v. See Brown v. Board of Education

Board of Education v. Pico, 76

Board of Regents, Keyishian v. See Keyishian v. Board of Regents

Book censorship, 136–138

Bork, Robert H., 127–130

Brandenburg v. Ohio (1969), 16, 112, 157, 158

Brennan, William, Jr., 27–28, 66–76, 87

Breyer, Stephen, 172, 183

Broadrick v. Oklahoma, 117, 122

Brody v. Spang, 97

Brown v. Board of Education, 63

Burnside v. Byars, 23, 25, 27, 28